Living Well in Retirement

Cynthia Yates

HARVEST HOUSE PUBLISHERS

EUGENE, OREGON

Published in association with the literary agency of Janet Kobobel Grant, Books & Such, 4788 Carissa Avenue, Santa Rosa, California 95405

This book is not intended to take the place of sound financial, medical, mental health, or any other professional advice. All opinions regarding food, medicine, alternative medicine, and pharmaceuticals should be regarded as the opinion of the author (unless otherwise cited) and may or may not be grounded in scientific fact. Neither the author nor the publisher assumes any liability for possible adverse consequences as a result of the information contained herein.

Cover by Terry Dugan Design, Minneapolis, Minnesota

Back cover photo by Kay Bjork

LIVING WELL IN RETIREMENT
Copyright © 2005 by Cynthia Yates
Published by Harvest House Publishers
Eugene, Oregon 97402
Library of Congress Cataloging-in-Publication Data
Yates, Cynthia, 1947–
  Living well in retirement / Cynthia Yates.
     p. cm.
  Includes bibliographical references.
  ISBN 0-7369-1583-4 (pbk.)
  1. Retirement. 2. Retirees—Psychology. 3. Retirees—Family relationships. 4. Retirees—Religious life. 5. Retirees—Life skills guides. 6. Older people—Life skills guides. I. Title.
  HQ1062.Y37 2005
  646.7'9—dc22   2004022266

Printed in the United States of America

05   06   07   08   09   10   / VP-CF /   10   9   8   7   6   5   4   3   2   1

To Wonder Man

*"Honey, I think you should write a book that offers
a little advice and a whole lot of comfort.
Yes. That's the kind of book I need right now."*

With gratitude, I acknowledge the following people
for their professional advice.
With joy, I thank them as friends.

Pamela Roberts Oehrtman, MD
Larry Clayton, DDS
Ryan M. Wigness, DC
Beth Morgenstern, AAMS
Rev. Mary Leach
Rev. Bill Baumgarten
Janis Krause, Newspaper Publisher

With humility, I thank my friend and agent,
Janet Kobobel Grant; Harvest House Publishers;
and my editor, Gene Skinner

Contents

1

A Wake-Up Call

CYNTHIA:

So Wonder Man retired. (My husband, Joe.) It was the moment we had waited for, daydreamed of, and worked toward. We both approached his retirement with enthusiasm, expecting togetherness, bliss, and freedom. We were greeted with confusion, frustration, and strife.

"What happened?" I blurted, my white-knuckled grip on the steering wheel even tighter as I swallowed deeply and barged into Kansas City traffic. We were headed east to join our son and his family for the winter. We were also heading into our new life. "Where did *we* go?" I cried.

I was bewildered and angry. This was supposed to be fun. You know—us. 24/7. I felt as if overnight and out of nowhere an Amtrak Superliner blasted by and creamed me. That's how abruptly our marriage seemed to change.

My husband—the man with whom I'd daydreamed for more than two decades—sulked in the passenger seat and let his body language speak for him. We were in for a *long* trip, as all of Interstate 70 loomed ahead.

JOE:

It had been a long career. I was not where I needed to be or wanted to be with the retirement thing, but there came a time to go. Cynicism had begun to creep into my daily life as a result of all the changes at the U.S. Forest Service, where I worked. They say a prophet can't go home, and 37 years in one spot was pretty much home. And then I left it to start a new life—just like that. But it wasn't that simple. The unknown was the hardest part for me.

Cynthia and I had been apart out of necessity for long periods of time throughout the previous three years. Suddenly we were together again—and she had all these plans, all these expectations. Whoopee.

As you will soon find out, I didn't exactly share my beloved's zeal for all the new experiences this transition brought.

Retired

A year has passed since my husband retired, and it has been a hard year. Our tempers have flared, we have tested our marital commitment, and we have bruised each other's egos as we two knuckleheads grappled with the emotional, physical, and financial fallout of retirement.

Our relationship has changed and continues to reshape itself with each new day. When Joe and I are fully engaged in the change that retirement continues to bring, we are usually responsible enough to direct it in a healthy and positive manner. When we are tired, poorly nourished, or in a personal snit, the change in our relationship brings tension and turbulence.

We thought we'd left some really hard issues way back in our past, but smoldering embers of discord that were never fully extinguished were easily inflamed once we added new fuel. And the stress that came with Joe's retirement was fuel enough to launch *Sputnik* back into orbit.

But my husband and I are also reestablishing the comfortable groove of friendship, familiarity, and intimacy. A fresh vitality, a certain kick, and a lighthearted giggle are slowly emerging from deep inside. We seem to be getting stronger, and we're willing to barge into heavy traffic with all four of our hands on the wheel even though we haven't a clue where we are headed. Retirement, after all, is uncharted territory. It is also extrabiblical in the sense that it is a historical concept, rather than a biblical one (except for God's specific instructions for Levites in Numbers 8:24-26). Certainly, aging and work and rest are perennial themes in all human societies, but retirement is a relatively new and unique notion. What does this social construct called retirement look like at the start of the twenty-first century? We shall soon see.

> There is no physical or psychological reason to choose 65 as a universal retirement age.

The Big Booming Picture

I'm a boomer, and chances are that you're a boomer. (Baby boomers were born between 1947 and 1954.) Retirement is upon you or is creeping close, and that is likely why you've picked up this book. What will retirement mean for you? Are you ready?

Sure I'm ready, the prepared ones say. *I have my retirement account and savings, the house is paid for, and the pantry is stocked. I dusted off my stack of books too, and I'm avidly watching the Travel Channel. Even bought a set of clubs. Yessirreebob! Ready? Ready, willing, and able!*

Not so fast. While some of you may think you are ready, you may not be ready at all. Let's take a look at the big picture.

Americans most often equate meaningful retirement with financial security, which for some is cause for genuine alarm. Some researchers claim that approximately 75 percent of boomers are not financially prepared for retirement.[1] Add to that the profound effect retirement has on relationships, the physical changes that come with aging, the sudden consequence of free time and leisure, and particularly for men, the loss of identity. Also, though retirement means leaving something behind and going forward, a new direction might mean looking backward to assess life and legacy or to recover lost dreams.

Retirement is fundamentally about managing various kinds of means to accomplish various kinds of ends. It is also about growing old, family, and the completion of life. This brings to mind biblical themes of stewardship, economy, vocation, wisdom, community, and eternity.

Several years ago the words *holistic health* hit the scene. Many of us scoffed. *"Mind-body-spirit" connection, indeed! Hand me my aspirin and go chew on tree bark, you weirdos!* We now know—scientifically—that emotion, spirituality, and life circumstance play as big a role in our well-being as exercise and avoidance of germs. All of these factors exhibit an inescapable interdependence, and frankly, by the time most of us hit our later years this interdependence is more acutely apparent. (Usually because our bodies refuse to function according to our whim and will.)

> Does not long life bring understanding?
>
> Job 12:12

Likewise, retirement has interdependent factors: financial, emotional, psychological, practical, and social. We will look at retirement holistically as we consider God's view of aging, retirement, work, and how this all jibes with popular culture. (Who knows? We may end up "retiring" the very notion of retiring!)

A Wake-Up Call

This first chapter has one major purpose: to act as a wake-up call. For some it will be a call to get a better grip on stewardship principles. For others it will be a call to reflect upon this mighty serious life passage. My hope for all is that it will be an eye-opener to the profound

Stump Time!

Since I am keen on writing hands-on books and like to prod my readers to action, *Living Well in Retirement* occasionally breaks with a call to Stump Time!

Some of you may be familiar with a sculpture by Rodin called *The Thinker.* It was all the rage back in the 60s: a serious fellow sitting on a pedestal contemplating life, chin resting on his fist. The "stump" is your pedestal, and Stump Time! is my encouragement that you contemplate certain issues in your own life. This may be through a specific written exercise, a little meditative soul-searching, or prayer.

Yet before any of this gets under way, I'd like to sound an alarm or two in hopes of alerting you to the necessity of contemplating retirement (without falling off your stump).

impact this transition can have upon you in some ways other than on your money market account. This is a transition, after all, to a life stage that itself orients you for your final passage.

And now, some facts (current in or before 2004).

Financial Oopsedness

- According to a 2004 Retirement Confidence Survey by the Employee Benefit Research Institute, 40 percent of Americans are doing nothing for retirement, and of the remaining, 60 percent have total assets of less than $25,000. Following conventional wisdom of withdrawing from your retirement nest egg at 4 percent each year, a $25,000 retirement fund provides an annual income of $1000. Oops.

- According to one guideline, if retirement is five years away, you should already have more than six times your current annual income invested.

- Three percent annual inflation is the historical average. So if you need $2500 a month in retirement, in 15 years you will need $3900 to keep the field level. Ah, but you might not live that long? Read on.

Reality Beckons

- Forty-five percent of people in today's workforce are concerned that they will live longer than their retirement nest egg. The average retirement lasts 25 years.

- The latest mortality rates show that men live, on average, to age 80 and women live to age 84. However, the fastest growing population segment in America includes people who are 85 or older, so people radically undervalue the possibility of living into their late 80s or 90s.

- In 2001, the median annual reported income of older persons was $14,152. The median annual income of older women was $11,313.

Hey, No Problem

When polled, high percentages of people insisted that they would continue to work, by either not retiring at all or by beginning a second career after retirement. (Current statistics diminish those hopes somewhat. Forty percent of workers retire earlier than planned, often due to job loss or declining health.) According to Alicia Munnell, director of the Center for Retirement Research at Boston College, postponing retirement by working two extra years can cut the amount needed to finance retirement by about 25 percent.

> Individuals of all ages are simply not financially prepared to meet the increasing costs of living longer.
>
> Marc E. Lackritz,
> *past president of Securities Industry Association*

Postretirement employment is a viable and necessary option for many people, and we will consider it again in this book. But how many jobs for the over-60 set will be available? To be fair, some analysts believe the ratio of workers to job openings will soon be so low that older, retired people may be tapped for their experience.

By 2030 there are expected to be 79 million senior citizens in America. In 2030, I will be 83. Where will I be? How will I feel? What will I be doing? What about you? What's that you say? You'll be comfortably collecting Social Security?

Social S…S…Security

By 2008 the baby boom generation will begin to tap into Social Security benefits. But in 2018, retirement benefits will begin costing more than payroll taxes bring in. Pundits, politicians, economists, and cartoonists all have

> **A**nything that scares them into thinking they are not getting Social Security is okay with me because that is a healthy fear.
>
> **Scott Adams,**
> *creator of* Dilbert

their own spin on how Social Security will or will not be viable in the future. Most advisers suggest that you should loosely expect benefits from Social Security while covering your bases elsewhere. And hey— you *can* pay for your retirement in other ways:

1. You can increase your chances of a comfortable and secure retirement by up to 50 percent if you don't have any kids.

2. You can increase your chances of a comfortable and secure retirement exponentially if you never, ever get sick.

Take Two Aspirin and Gulp!

According to an article in *Parade,* one in three workers who lose their jobs also lose their health coverage,[2] and if you don't have adequate health insurance, your retirement savings can be wiped out in the blink of an eye. (Health insurance is covered in chapter 7.)

In its "Profile of Older Americans: 2002," the Administration on Aging (U.S. Department of Health and Human Services) cites that in the year 2000, older consumers averaged $3493 in out-of-pocket health care expenditures. The out-of-pocket health expense does not reflect nursing home care. The risk of a 65-year-old entering a nursing home in the future is 35 percent. In the year 2003, the average cost of the average person in an average nursing home was approximately $66,000 each year.

It Went By So Fast!

Crept up on you, didn't it? Planning for retirement way back when you entered the work force just had to wait.

First came the new car, then the honeymoon, the house, the other new car, the kids, braces, the boat, the minivan, vacations, Christmas presents, dance lessons, tuition. Besides, it wasn't fair. Why was the burden of your future suddenly thrust on your shoulders like a 60-pound backpack? Your generation was coping with new realities, one of which was job security—or the lack of it. What happened to job security, to benefits, and to our confidence in Social Security?

I'm Not Prepared!

As we boomers banged into a sweeping change of reality, we were never coached, taught, or prepared for retirement years. And why should we have been? Our parents and aunts and uncles never prepared. They just went to work every day, retired, collected their pensions, and took off in their RVs. But us? Suddenly we find ourselves maneuvering down potholed roads, far from the four-laners we were accustomed to cruising, nary a road map in sight, with warning signs everywhere:

> *Warning:* Huge Change Ahead
> *Caution:* Emotional Detours Around the Corner
> *Slow Down:* Financial Potholes in Pavement
> *Yield:* Merge with Aging Body
> *Prepare to Stop:* Relational Flagman

Relax

We are going to tackle this complex issue of retirement head-on, book in hand—your road map for the best years of your life. In spite of this chapter's wake-up call, retirement is the time to fling that alarm clock out the window, is it not? Here, at long last, is better news:

Retirement need not be a scary time at all. Retirement may be uncharted, but it offers the potential to be the journey of a lifetime if you are well-equipped when you start. If you are retired already, consider this a short break where you stock a few necessary supplies for the rest of your trip. And no matter where you are in this journey, feel free to ask directions.

The Payoff

Living well in retirement—a mighty appealing sentiment. Maybe even a burst of bravado in the face of all those statistics. Yet we all want to live well in retirement, and why shouldn't we? We've worked hard all our lives. We've dragged ourselves out of bed on freezing mornings, scraped snow off windshields with broom handles, turned the ignition key with frozen fingers, and begged for the motor to start. We've drunk tepid coffee from moldy mugs, crammed through turnstiles, and shoved our way onto commuter trains and buses. We've stared endlessly into a computer monitor, slid under houses to fix pipes, driven a million miles. We've been punctual, efficient, successful, and compliant. All of this, mind you, for the day we could retire. Retirement! How we want to live it our way, and how we want to live it well!

You *should* live well in retirement. But what does that mean?

2

What's It All About, Alfie?

CYNTHIA:

Joe Yates. By the time he retired after 37 years with the U.S. Forest Service, his name evoked respect and admiration for his accomplishments in reforestation and contract administration. Joe's long tenure at the Swan Lake Ranger District had many rewards. His career lasted long enough for him to see established stands of 40-foot timber where he once supervised the planting of seedlings in land that had been clear-cut or scarred by fire.

From the moment I met Joe until a day in early October of 2003, his retirement loomed as a future triumph, totally surreal but somewhat scripted. Joe envisioned retirement as we all used to—living in relative comfort, traveling a bit, and spending most days in an aluminum fishing boat. Retirement meant this: After punching the clock every day and doing good work, he would settle securely into his future. The only formal plan attached to retirement was covered by the word *benefits.* Joe entered government service at a time when people tolerated lower pay during a career because of benefits. They presumed, of course, that in exchange for faithful work they would be vested and secure, just like everyone before them. After all, the retirees at the old-timers' picnics held by the Forest Service had big smiles, RV's...and aluminum fishing boats.

JOE:

Cynthia's got it pretty much right. My plans from early on were that when I was eligible to retire I would. As the time approached I began to shuffle exact dates, consider what they meant to the whole picture, and try to figure out how I was going to compensate for our lifestyle and still retire. I suppose you could say the closer I got to retirement age, the closer I got to reality. But reality didn't always square with my dreams. Some dreams were abandoned, some were postponed. I still look at the classified ads for that aluminum fishing boat.

What's It All About, Alfie?

If you can recall the lyrics to that song, belt them out. For the life of me, I can't...though I remember the words seemed fatalistic and very existential: We live, we die, life happens, why bother? In this chapter, I will give my answer to what it's all about as I define critical terminology that is central to this book. What is retirement about? How do we develop a good enough attitude to live well during retirement? And while we're at it, what does "living well" mean, anyway?

A Short History

As previously mentioned, the Bible offers no specific warrant for retirement as we know it. From Genesis on, God calls mankind to work. Through our toil we are to steward creation, to enter into human fellowship and interdependence, to create community, and to serve others. How do you retire from that? Well, we found a way...

According to Christine Price, "The role of 'retiree' and the stage of 'retirement' we identify with today is a socially constructed concept that was created as a result of the passage of the Social Security Act in 1935."[1] The intent was to stimulate the economy by offering older workers some financial incentive to leave the workforce and make way for younger workers. Retirement has become normative—and anticipated—ever since.

The Event

One dictionary calls retirement the "state of being retired." *There's* a helpful definition! We will all retire someday, but for now, we have differing expectations of what the actual event will look like. Whether you call it retirement, "re-hirement," or "free-tirement," not all retirements are created equal. Some are planned retirements and some are unplanned, some are full-time retirements and some are part-time, some are voluntary retirements and some are involuntary.

> Retirement is a fluke of the twentieth century. For people who are active and healthy, it is destructive.
>
> **David Ekerdt,**
> *University of Kansas Gerontology Center*

Lots of us put in our time, and when our time is up, off we go, clutching a Certificate of Service and a fistful of retirement cards and gag jokes. The countdown during our final year of service is chock-full of anticipation, some regret, and even a bit of "short timer's" attitude. We have time to begin the transition and the adjustment. (We might even read a book or two about what's ahead.) Joe and I were fortunate to go to a government-sponsored retirement seminar, during which I made two distinct observations: (1) Most of us in the room stared at the presenters with a look of sheer naïveté, and (2) I was already tallying numbers in my head and concluding that my husband couldn't *think* about retiring until he was approximately 97 years old. (Part-time postretirement work has since opened new possibilities for advancement and growth in Joe's life. The assurance of his new part-time work garnered, admittedly, a giant sigh of relief from me.)

Some positions, occupations, or careers have a ceiling. Mandatory retirement due to age can come when a person feels at the top of his or her game, and it can be a bitter pill to swallow. Regardless, out you go—suddenly disenfranchised from the security you have created for yourself, standing out in the parking lot while some upstart takes your place.

In increasingly more cases, for many thousands of workers in today's reality, retirement is anything but planned. It is often the result of downsizing, corporate takeover or restructuring, or corporate failure or duplicity. Occasionally it is the outcome of family circumstance or failing health. I admit that I cannot begin to understand the depth of bitterness, betrayal, insecurity, and uncertainty these workers and their families must endure. I can only hope that this book will offer some counsel and provide hope for a better day.

One way or another, planned or unplanned, voluntary or involuntary, full-time or part-time, more than 76 million baby boomers and others are either facing retirement, or have already begun it. What does that mean?

While Wonder Man has his own variation to this theme, which you will read about later, I have broken the word in half:

Retire...

Simple enough: To retire is to withdraw from, to remove oneself, to go away, to move on. There are a few distinctions to this going away and moving on:

- To retire is to move from your middle-adult years into what is now popularly called your "third age."

- To retire is to lay tracks for your next future.

- To retire is *not* to hit the end of the road. It is to take another road, one you've never traveled.

- To retire as we have known it (as it was in our parents' generation) is for the most part no longer practical—or probable.

...*ment*

What does that mean? That four-letter suffix gets attached to a whole lot of words: postponement, engagement, enjoyment, encouragement, fulfillment.

I learned that when it is attached to words it indicates a "resulting state or action." When we attach *ment* to retire, we are in (or planning to be in) a state of going away and moving on. Think of yourself as taking a turn off the interstate and continuing down a brand new road in a strange new land.

Even if you're on the right track, you'll get run over if you sit still.

Retirement is a dynamic word, always on the go. With that in mind, I decided to use *ment* as an acronym. A funny little acronym, and a really busy little acronym: maximize, engage, nourish, and tag along. These four terms will be like the tires on a car that takes you into the rest of your life.

M—Maximize

E—Engage

N—Nourish

T—Tag along

Maximize

It is a super feeling to know that you can siesta when you choose (sleep will be addressed in chapter 7) or that you can enjoy doing absolutely nothing. I passionately believe that our society has overlooked the wise use of leisure. Slacking off from time to time is healthy. However...

If you are retired, you are probably free from the bonds of a certain routine, order, or protocol that kept you in lockstep for most of your life. You may never before have had the opportunity or the freedom to grab life with gusto. That opportunity is in your hands this very moment. You are not dead. Not yet, anyway. Whether you are physically mobile or not, you can still grab life and do-si-do. Don't waste the opportunity of each new sunrise. No matter the chore or challenge ahead, maximize the experience and the potential of each new day. You are bound to have tough days, but they may be easy compared to the hardships life has already flung your way. Now that you are older and wiser and can better understand the value and meaning of life, make the most of it. Maximize the use of your five senses: see, speak, touch, smell, and hear with more resolve and awareness while you minimize your daily stress.

Engage

You simply must engage with others after you have retired.

I know. You may want to lock your front door and throw away the key. You may need a break from the demands or nasty personalities of people who were integrated into your career. Taking a rest or a break is probably smart. Just don't drop out. Some of you—you know who you are—have become so burned-out that goldfish are all the company you can bear. I understand. But may I ask, how can you contribute to the kingdom of God in an easy chair? Oh, but you've retired! From God? No can do. Needless to say, your primary engagement should be in earnest conversation with Him.

> Nobody grows old merely by living a number of years. We grow old by deserting our ideals. Years may wrinkle the skin, but to give up enthusiasm wrinkles the soul.
>
> **Samuel Ullman**

Find others with whom to engage, not just for God's good pleasure, but for your health as well. (Rumor has it that those of us who maintain friends and have some socialization [Pat Sajak and Vanna White excluded] are healthier and live longer.) People who are older than you, younger than you, less mentally developed than you, or in poorer health than you would appreciate your smile. The smiles you get in return will add immeasurably to the quality of your retirement!

Nourish

Maintaining good health by nourishing mind, body, and spirit is critical for moving on.

Are you creeping closer to that magic retirement date, or have you hit it, only to have a body that will no longer heed your beck and call? Do you have feet that hurt too much to walk the steps of Cinque Terre? A mind too befuddled to concentrate on the photography class you planned to take? A spirit that is broken and in ruins and that keeps you at arm's length from the One who loves you?

At our advancing age we must step up to the plate once and for all and develop healthy habits that will carry us into our remaining years (which statistics show may be plentiful). Resolve to nourish your body, mind, and spirit. It is never too late. Never. Turn yourself into the project you've ignored for too long.

Tag Along

Huck Finn and Tom Sawyer. Lewis and Clark. Adventurers. Explorers.

Being free to explore, to go with the flow, to walk off in the wood just to be—the joys are endless. These are some of the bonuses that come from a lifetime of work well done.

We've all heard the expression "Let go and let God." I want to add to that: "Let go and let music, let art, let laughter, let full moons, let forests, let streambeds, let trolley cars, let sidewalks, let others, let cocker spaniels, let grandchildren, let wind, let snow...."

You may take a while to find your rhythm, but give yourself time to tag along in life and see where you go.

Sorry, Tried All That

Maximize each day? I tried! I felt so lost, so out of place. I sat in my shop and bawled my head off. (Turn to chapter 6.)

Engage who? I tried! My partner in marriage and in life suddenly acts more like a stranger! (See chapter 5.)

Nourish my body? I tried! I just can't get a grip...my body feels like it's breaking down. (Chapter 7.)

Tag along, my foot! I tried! I sat under a tree and waited for something to move me. About all that moved was my hand swatting mosquitoes. (Try citrus essential oil—and keep reading.)

It Takes You to Tango

Retirement might not be what you thought it would be. Yet. Look at it this way: Retirement is a lot like marriage. Both bride and groom go into marriage starry-eyed, filled with notions of what this ideal time in their life will be, only to find marriage can only be comprehended from the inside out. Life has a way of leveling its own playing field. John Lennon said it well: "Life is what happens when you are busy making plans." (And I would add, when you are busy dreaming.)

For instance, marriage certainly brought you a few surprises, one of which was your powerlessness to make it perfect, in spite of any resolve. There was that *other person*, you know. Drat if that *other person* didn't sabotage your finest intentions. *She* or *he* was not supposed to react to you that way—it was not at all as you'd dreamed.

> **W**hat lies behind us and what lies before us are tiny matters compared to what lies within us.
>
> Oliver Wendell Holmes

In spite of that, and though challenging, for most of us marriage has been fulfilling, rewarding, and right. For others, though never married, or if theirs has ended in dissolution, marriage is usually still considered the ideal.

What's this got to do with retirement? The *other person* in retirement, the one who goes into it starry-eyed and filled with notions of how ideal a time it will be, the one who has the potential to sabotage the finest intentions—that *other person* is often you.

Sure, you may have no control over some circumstances: The bona fide demands or needs of others and your own failing health are two that come to mind. But the one character who can make or break your retirement experience is staring at this page.

A Mighty Important Attitude

Absolutely nothing will work successfully if we don't have the right attitude. I've written extensively about the impact attitude has on our lives, and this is a good place for a refresher.

Our attitude is a composite of our personality, our life experience, our worldview, and our spiritual maturity. Our sin nature also has a hand in this. Make no mistake: How we react to *everything* is governed and shaped by attitude. How we view what we possess, our work, and how we spend our time becomes part of who we are and is manifested by our attitude.

New stage, not old age.

You may have had so many disappointments throughout life that your attitude is pessimistic, sour grapes, or just indifferent to potentially exciting change or even the most auspicious events. Why get excited about something that may result in failure? Why dream if dreams do not come true? Why laugh when someone, somewhere, sooner or later, will poke fun at you or turn your smile upside down?

You may have been hurt so often when you've trusted friendship or love that you've learned not to extend your hand for anything but change at the grocery checkout. Besides, you've held your emotions inside for so long that arthritis has hardened your heart bones from lack of use. Engage with others? Hurts too much even to try.

Or you may have been catered to and given so much freedom as a youngster that you've grown to expect and demand the spotlight. The chip on your shoulder is the size of a toaster oven by now because of the disappointment and hurt piled high from a world that refused to oblige your every whim.

You may just be the type who looks at the glass of water as half empty. Your natural response may be to find reason for worry and to envision the worst possible scenario. You may have nary a positive spin in sight. That would be Wonder Man:

"Ohmygosh, Joseph! Look at the fabulous sunrise!"

"Yep, it's neat. I better get busy before it gets too hot." Or, "You never know—it could rain." Or, "A Volkswagen could fall out of the sky and flatten us at any time."

For the half-empty, worrier type, few things in life evoke passion or exuberance. (The flip side of this is quite plain: Life is safe, stable, and has no surprises.)

Or, you may be the type who looks at the glass as half full. You may even look at an *empty* glass with optimism, fairly trembling with excitement over what you can fill it with. That would be me:

"Cynthia, a Volkswagen just landed in our front yard."

"Ohmygosh, Joseph! Let's build a picket fence around it and plant petunias and turn it into a pond. Goldfish! I've always wanted gold-fish! And lily pads!"

For the half full, exuberant type, few things in life are boring or predictable. (The flip side of this fervor is this: When we encounter insurmountable difficulties, we are unprepared to cope emotionally, and we are often devastated when others aren't caught up in our enthusiasm.)

Half empty or half full, mind-sets influence us in subtle ways. Let's look at a simple change in weather patterns as an example.

Half Empty

What began as a stunning summer day has turned ugly. The sky is crowded with dark clouds and wind is coming your way—gale force, hurricane wind for sure. You look helplessly at the nylon canopy you just erected over your favorite garden spot. Its four stakes seem to be holding the metal frame, but the canopy heaves and flat-tens, heaves and flattens, like a balloon when it's pushed to its breaking point and then suddenly expels its air. Thoughts of chasing a ripped and tattered nylon tarp all over the neighborhood sour your mood. The canopy will undoubtedly be torn to shreds, and you're already anticipating the unpleasant task of returning that piece of junk to the store where you bought it. Expecting an argument from the courtesy desk at Shoptilyoudrop, you begin to practice your battle with some unknown and hapless clerk—out loud. All this while you stare out the window and wait for the certain destruction of not just your canopy but also the remains of what began as a stunning day.

Half Full

You are concerned that the canopy you bought may not weather the storm. After all, it looks so awesome over the wildflower garden and has provided shade for your wonderfully beat-up Adirondack chair, creating a favorite resting spot. You can't do anything but watch through the window. The wind is ferocious; if the canopy weathers this storm it will weather anything. You are glad you invested a little more money for good quality. You pour yourself an iced tea, pull up a chair, and thoroughly enjoy the spectacle as the storm pushes and heaves against the canopy. *Go canopy!*

Which Are You?

Half empty or half full? In spite of your answer, I have a news flash: You are old enough, experienced enough, sensible enough, and honest enough to improve your attitude. This is an important point because I rather doubt you want to stand in the way of the fulfillment of your own retirement years! You've waited too long and worked too hard. Pour some stability *and* enthusiasm into your glass and have a swig every morning. Call it your daily tonic. (Read about the Yates' daily tonic in chapter 7.)

Retirement is a profoundly awesome life change. It is a time of unlimited and unprecedented opportunity. Start it out right. Be sure you have a healthy, realistic, and enterprising attitude going in. Starting today, starting now, vow that you will retire from work (and eventually from this life) with gusto, with purpose, and with expectation. Pledge now to live life fully in retirement, and to do your best to live it well.

Living Well

What *is* this all about, Alfie? How do we live well?

For just about all of us, to live well is what we want, and many of us don't want much, at that. To be financially secure, to have reasonably good health, for family to be well and on speaking terms, to take pleasure in grandchildren, to keep busy (maybe through continued work of some sort), to be able to enjoy a little golf or fishing, to play bridge each week, to sleep in, perhaps to travel a little, to do good. Yes, that would be nice. Maybe to get away from the snow in the winter...yeah, throw that in. Oh—and the lawn...someone else to mow the lawn. Maybe get rid of the lawn altogether.

> All of you want to do well. But if you do not do good, too, then doing well will never be enough.
>
> Anna Quindlen

That is actually quite nice. Hardly a soul would not want that kind of retirement. I surmise this protocol would be on the wish list for anyone, regardless of income, whether a CEO of a Fortune 500 or someone who waited tables for 40 years. To all retirees, that would sure be having it all and living well. Spot-on! Sign me up.

Hold your horses.

"Having it all" may not rank as high as we think in the "life well lived" category. We intuitively know that a life well lived, a successful life, has little to do with material gain, prominence among others, or the comfortable perks of retirement.

The kind of living well I am talking about is more than personal ease. The kind of living well I am talking about is impossible to understand unless you identify with the cross of Christ.

To live well in or through any life passage means one single thing: to live according to God's purpose for your life.

When I am able to live according to His purpose, to recognize that regardless of my circumstance I have relinquished control to Him (not lip service), then I am able to connect with the joy that reality brings.

Joy in the face of adversity, in the face of triumph, in the face of failing health, in the face of everything—including retirement.

Living life according to God's purpose does not disregard anyone's wish list (though for some it may alter the outcome dramatically!). Living according to His purpose brings meaning to our lives, provides a feeling of fulfillment at our deepest levels, and creates in us an impression of wonderment and trust. Living according to His purpose also means getting lost.

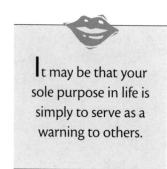

It may be that your sole purpose in life is simply to serve as a warning to others.

Get Lost

Christians have long promoted the notion of dying to self, much to the irritation of others.

"Nonsense!" the world yells. "You want to live well? Start by loving yourself. You are supposed to love yourself before you can even begin to love others. You are supposed to look out for number one!"

"Not so!" says Christ. "The way to life is to deny yourself, to take up your cross, and to follow Me."

"Oh, for heaven's sake," blurt our exasperated friends. "Will you get off this 'cross' kick?"

"No can do, no want to do," says the disciple of Christ, "I will not—for heaven's sake."

Look. Christians talk about dying to self for good cause. If we die to self, we get out of the way and let God the Holy Spirit have His way with us. I don't know about you, but if God is real—and I believe He is—I'd much rather have Him guiding my actions than muddle through on my own. And so would you, if you're honest. You and I both know how often we've gotten our rudders stuck in the mud banks of our latest fiascos. No, I'd rather lose myself to a holy God who has a purpose for my life.

What? God has a purpose for my life? You better believe it! You think He just uses saints and martyrs and pastors to advance His kingdom?

You think the only reason you are here is to go through the motions? Step, step, step—get born, grow up, work. Step, step, step—raise kids, retire, fish, play cards, die. Pul-leeze! This is a good place to rephrase what John Lennon said: *God* is what happens when you get out of the way while you are busy making plans.

How can any of us, at any age, ever retire from God's purpose for our lives? Yet what do we say? We raised good kids and put in 40 years of honorable work, and now we're scot-free? I'm not so sure.

Raising kids and working honorably may have been an important part of His purpose, but no one's worldly mission is over until someone throws a shovel of dirt over his or her cold, tired bones. I'm not so sure we can take a vacation from vocation. We just need to tag along and get out of the way.

Excellent models for this are Jimmy and Rosalynn Carter. Jimmy Carter was president of the United States. (You could certainly call *that* a purposeful life!) He and his wife, Rosalynn, have gone into their retirement with apparent obedience and surrender to Christ and with servants' hearts that could put many of us to shame. We commonly see President Carter's picture in a newspaper, straddling a floor joist, hammer in hand, as he labors for Habitat for Humanity. Or we read that both he and Rosalynn are on a mission to help the disadvantaged someplace in the world. (I'd wager a bowl of peanuts that President and Mrs. Carter would say their life is full and blessed, and that they are moving on.)

> For it is by grace you have been saved, through faith—and this not from yourselves, it is the gift of God—not by works, so that no one can boast. For we are God's workmanship, created in Christ Jesus to do good works, *which God prepared in advance for us to do.*
>
> **Ephesians 2:8-10**
> *(emphasis added)*

Stump Time!

What was prepared in advance for you to do? What is your strength? What is your love? What is your gift? What is your talent? What makes you smile? What makes you cry? What makes you feel alive? That is your purpose—the driveshaft to your life. Doesn't it follow that you should lose yourself to God so He can direct that purpose to His glory?

A good way to find the answers to the questions posed in "Stump Time!" is to look over your shoulder and discover what you may have left behind as you marched ever forward throughout your career.

3

It's All Behind You Now

CYNTHIA:

A peek into the past....

Two months after Joe's fifth birthday, the phone rang in his mother's beauty shop in Shelby, Montana. Crammed into what once was the family's living room and dining room, Mama's shop was home to clusters of hair-dryer chairs covered in turquoise naugahyde, perm rods piled high in wheeled bins, a rust-stained corner sink, and a footpath worn into a swirly black-and-white linoleum floor. The stinging smell of permanent wave lotion drifted through an open door into the family's small living quarters, an odor strong enough to make a grown man cry. Yet Mama was the one who cried into the phone that day in March so long ago. Joseph's father was dead.

Killed in a head-on collision on the Eastern Montana prairie, Joseph Percival Yates left behind a woman with a beauty shop and a fatherless boy who became a man that very day.

The Modern Beauty Shop became Mama's sanctuary and her salvation. Her husband's death benefit was barely enough for the funeral. The Modern Beauty Shop became the place where Joe would report as he dutifully faced responsibilities that came with sudden manhood— including providing emotional support for his mother. The single most important male role model in his life was snatched from him, and now he would learn to negotiate life alone and by gut feelings. Joseph William Yates became old before he was young.

Mama did her best to instill ethics and virtue into her only child, the local Lutheran church drummed it all home, and Joe's innate sense of fairness and integrity helped him along the way. His life was not without blunder, scraped knees, bruised ego, or the insecurity that haunts him to this day.

"You know, Cynthia," he said recently, "I never quite understood my insecurity until lately. I mean, I kissed someone I loved goodbye in the morning, and he never came home at night."

Joe:

A lot of memories still remain from March of 1953. One vivid memory is when I got Belle.

My dad died on Monday, but the Friday night before, he called from the warehouse and told my mom to send me the half block to Main Street, where he would meet me. He had a surprise. He'd brought home a dog, a two-year-old female Doberman pinscher named Belle.

A few days after my dad died my dog got out into the street. She was playing with another dog when a driver intentionally ran them both over. I went bawling into the house: My dog is dead! She's gone to heaven, Mama! Just like my dad!

Just like my dad. I may have been five, but I knew my dad was never coming home again. Life changed for me, and Belle (who actually survived to live a long life) became my constant companion.

Little do I know how life would have been different if my father had lived longer, but I'm sure I would have been a lot more regimented and structured. I ran amok from time to time; I became a "self-made man." My mom saw that I received a lot of male influence—and if they weren't there I would find some on my own. But the loving guidance was missing. My dad was dead.

Only by God's grace have I made it this far with a family and with people who love me.

What You Left Behind

Without question, the tragic death of Joe's father had an impact on my husband's emotions and behavior as he negotiated life essentially alone. Our life experience can have a huge impact on our attitudes. In other words, a person's temperament may not be the only reason he or she sees a glass as half empty. Life happens.

Life happens all day long, every day, and it can add upset or joy to daily routine, to plans, and to dreams. Life especially happens during transitions, and boy oh boy, is retirement one big transition!

For us boomers, retirement poses the hardest transition within our life experience. Other transitions (the draft, marriage, children) certainly challenged us, but as a demographic group we were so absorbed with wildly changing societal standards throughout the past 40 years that we were simply too swept away by life to notice challenge. For many of us, the last four decades are a blur.

Yet we weren't exactly guileless during our generation's march through time. After all, we gave rise to the turbulent '60s, slid through the rather innocuous '70s, and became avid devotees of the "Me" decade of the '80s as cultural values shifted, practically making it our civic duty to connect with our individual selves and declare our independence from traditional mores. We bought into the paradigm that personal fulfillment was our right, and we appropriated the national imperative to do our own thing in our own way. Yet somewhere along the way we failed to grasp basic skills in household economics or simple stewardship principles. We were too busy living in the moment.

We can, however, happily claim one sweet period in our pasts, and that is our early childhood, something we left behind long, long ago.

Most of us zipped through childhood playing marbles and chasing cousins with half-lit sparklers on the Fourth of July. We drank our weight in Kool-Aid and were overcome by our good fortune when we had chocolate milk for lunch. We hit preteen years with the early Barbie and BB guns, and we counted the days until we would be old enough to have our very own madras shirt or blouse—and drive! (That is, if the "old man" would let us borrow the family station wagon.)

We were teens with the Beach Boys, Neil Sedaka, and the Beatles, many of us blissfully ignorant of the profound political, cultural, and global changes happening around us. Then came college or a job or marriage. Kids. Cars. Mortgages. Swoosh. Just like that: swoosh. We rarely had time to think.

But now it's different. With retirement looming, we're taking time to think about what we're doing and to ponder what's ahead. We want to get this right. That is what this book is all about. Yet before we step too decisively into our nebulous future, let's glance back and consider what we have left behind. First we'll look at our childhood dreams, and then we'll consider our adult attachment to work.

Lost in Reverie

Childhood Awe

We once exhibited a sweet innocence and delight in the amazing world around us. Some of us still do—maybe you smiled when you read about sparklers on the Fourth of July.

For the most part, we boomers had charmed childhoods. Before the technological assault, we enjoyed a happy, dirty-fingernail, mosquito-bitten, frozen-toe simplicity to life and play. We spent half our lives outdoors with nothing more than a bike, an old inner tube, a spoon to dig with, and a pile of dirt. We played outside until it was too dark to see, and it was all very wonderful.

We were part of the outdoors, part of creation, and we played in perfect harmony on the beach, in the forests, on the plains, or in a tree. We chased butterflies, collected bugs, and filled aluminum pie tins with moss and colored stones.

Holidays held special court with us. Easter, in particular, was a time of renewal. New outfits, shoes, and socks were left untouched in brown paper department-store bags and stowed in a closet until that special day. We took a ritual cleansing bath before donning our Easter finery. Our parents, the house, and the car were all as clean as were we.

Thanksgiving, Christmas, family reunions, picnics, stores closed on Sunday, church on Sunday…we were impressionable and filled with wonder, as children should be.

But eventually life crept in to subdue much of that awe. And as we became more practiced at life, as we began to tenuously take control, to light the sparklers ourselves, to pay for the Easter clothes, and to plan the family picnics, we grew a little numb, anesthetized and inoculated from our youthful wonder. We had to grow up.

To grow up we had to have the awe punched out of us. Certainly, we couldn't approach life's responsibilities with the mind of an eight-year-old. Yet how sweet it would be if we had the gumption to play marbles again, or to stay outside until it was too dark to see.

One of my favorite prayers from *The Book of Common Prayer* addresses this:

> Almighty and everlasting God, you made the universe with all its marvelous order, its atoms, worlds, and galaxies, and the infinite complexity of living creatures: Grant that, as we probe the mysteries of your creation, we may come to know you more truly, and more surely fulfill our role in your eternal purpose; in the name of Jesus Christ our Lord. Amen.

Stump Time!

When I was a child, _____.

I still _____

_____

All I Have to Do Is Dream

That's what the Everly Brothers sang: Dream, dream, dream.

Joe's high school dream was to retire young and wealthy. He had it all planned back then: to get a good paying job (what it was didn't matter) and retire after he made $25,000 for five years in a row. By then he would have a big house with a swimming pool and a circular bed. (He still remembers the dimensions of his dream retirement house. [This must be a guy thing.] The roof was 120 feet by 80 feet, the house itself was 80 feet by 40 feet, and it had a full basement.)

I'd given some thought to being a millionaire by the time I was 35. Pretty naïve and downright materialistic for the both of us.

Frankly, my thoughts were really just talk. I didn't actually dream about my future. And realistic, measurable goals? Forgetaboutit! *The measurements of a future house?* Oh, please. I look back at my early adult years and see only a clueless, drifting, young woman.

When I think hard (I have to dig very, very deeply), I can find a dream way back, one that was shoved aside and covered with mountains of dust and debris: When I was little I wanted more than anything to live on a farm with chickens, feather beds, and slamming screen doors. I wanted this farm to come equipped with a grandmother who made lemon meringue pies and a grandfather who harnessed a team of horses for hayrides. I wanted gardens filled with berries and corn on the cob, and the sweet smell of hay and molasses everywhere. Mostly I desperately wanted those grandparents, and I wanted them to love me dearly. That was my dream, the dream I left behind. What was your dream?

Stump Time!

My dream was_____.

I realized my dream because_____.

I never realized my dream because_____.

Think hard. Pry open those closed doors to your memory and blow away some dust. Be a kid again. Dream on. Dream, dream, dream.

The Mundane

Several aspects of your life either disappear or don't come with you when you retire. Such matters as identity and esteem come to mind, as do power, authority, and control; financial and emotional security; routine and predictability; and daily hassles. You also leave behind a legacy.

Identity and Esteem

Who are you? Who are you going to be? For my two cents, your answer should be as ambiguous as those questions. "I dunno" would fit nicely here.

Keeping in mind that I haven't a whit of training in psychology, I feel we should always be a bit muddled insofar as who we are and who we are going to be—apart from the identity we find in Christ, that is.

We can look back every single day to evaluate and discover who we were yesterday. But today? Today is still happening! It's too soon to know who we are today. And tomorrow? You've got to be kidding.

Okay. I can nail down a few things. Today, at this minute, I am a follower of Jesus Christ, a wife, a mother, a mother-in-law, a grandmother, a daughter, a sister, an aunt, a friend. I am Polish and French with a smidgen of German. I am of a certain age, with varying shades of hair color and undisclosed weight. I live *(yes!)* on a small farm in

Montana (no chickens yet) with feather beds and a screen door that slams. And I am an author.

If I stopped writing tomorrow, I would scratch "author" off my bio, "ex-author" sounding rather silly. I am sure I'd replace author with something else, like explorer. I love to explore.

Joe can no longer say he is a silvicultural technician or a contracting officer's representative for the United States Forest Service. So he's replaced those words with "part-time contracting instructor." He's also added a few more words to his bio: shepherd (we have sheep), full-time grandpa (when the grandkids are around), and retiree.

Certainly, Joe's sense of identity took a hit. For heaven's sake, he evolved into his position with the government over a 37-year period that fed his personal esteem and gave him purpose. That can be a hard act to replace. But replace it he must. The risk is too great if he doesn't.

What risk? Let's get real: I've gone to a lot of retirement parties over the course of Joseph's career. I've seen some retirees head off into the sunset with wide grins and a happy future. I've also seen a few who could not leave, returning to the office regularly, keeping close tabs on policies and procedures—even obsessing over those policies (That's not the way *we* did it!") to the point of outright activism and annoyance. Where is the life? It is a life stuck by a bungee cord to a past that is over. That's why it's called *past*.

past \'past\ : gone by in time; belonging to, having existed or occurred in time previous to this

I've also seen some people slip into depression and become virtual prisoners of their safe environs (in front of the TV or in the shop). One woman remarked to me, "Phil was depressed for a year after he retired." Curiously, Phil also suffered from a serious illness that manifested itself about that time. Any association? Your guess is as good as mine.

Look. You are not who you were yesterday. Get on with life. A lot of it is still out there to be lived. For now, give yourself a new identity!

I am always enchanted by names of Native Americans: "Walks at Night," "Sees Many Stars," or "Speaks with Wind." (I suppose my given name might be "Works with Words.") Take your cue from this and call

Stump Time!

My name for myself as I begin to develop a new identity
is_____

_____.

yourself "Man (or Woman) Who Is About to Bloom." Makes me think
of our perennial garden.

Did you know that when a perennial plant is young, hardly a
bloom is to be seen? As the plant gets older, it develops a strong root
system, thick stems or branches, and mighty pretty flowers.

Power, Authority, and Control

You've lost your power, authority, control, and seniority. It may be
that all you have to control these days is a house on a lot with a small
yard and a few trees. Yippee skippee. Have you considered that your
job right now might be to direct your efforts into stewarding that
property that the Lord has put in your care?

What's that you say? *You* are the one who schlepped to work—and
worked hard you did—to get that property? Bushwah. If you think
you alone have put yourself in the driver's seat, you really do need to
sit on that stump someplace and contemplate God's grace.

What's that you say? "God's grace, my eye?" So you did it all
through your own blood, sweat, and tears, did you? Tell me—how
come you weren't born in an impoverished country under a dictator?
How come you have benefited from relatively good health that has
enabled you to work? How come you can slip between clean sheets on
a cushy mattress at night rather than huddle under a bridge in a
packing crate? God's grace, my friend. *Why* God has been so gracious
to you and me while others suffer is another book entirely. I just want
to get this straight right now: God's providence and grace are working
in our lives even when we are not consciously aware of them, or consciously falling on our faces before Him in humility. To God be the
power and the authority and the control—and the seniority.

Stump Time!

What am I trying to control? _____.

Whom am I trying to control? _____.

Is this healthy or destructive? _____.

If you have been in a position of power most of your career, you may consider these comments as trite, naïve, or even offensive. In a sense, they may be. I imagine it would be challenging to awaken one morning without an army to command. To be just another person waiting in line at the bakery without a platoon of subservients to salute you might be a difficult adjustment. You need a stump.

Financial and Emotional Security

Have you left your financial and emotional security behind? Life can be a scary place when you feel insecure, especially when it comes to finances! With some grit and determination, you can flip your insecurities inside out. You are not alone—countless books on the subject of money (including a few of my own) or emotional health offer considerable help.

> Work furnishes a sense of place and membership in a valued community.
>
> Leaving a job involves more than simply ceasing to work.
>
> **Nancy K. Schlossberg**

For many of you, the bald reality is that you have not prepared quite well enough to feel confident about finances in retirement. You are facing the loss of certainty of a steady paycheck. That does not mean for a second that you can't live well. It may just mean a change in behavior, in lifestyle, or in spending habits.

The next chapter is dedicated to the issue of retirement and finance. For now, let me say this, no matter how Pollyanna you may think it sounds: Sunsets, walks on the beach, hikes in the mountains, music on the radio, and the smiles of passersby cost little to nothing.

What about the emotional security you left behind? Friends in the workplace are hard to beat. They probably know more about you than your immediate family—maybe more than your mate! Think about it. Though this is becoming less common, you may have been in the company of a certain handful of folks for a long time. You have grown old together, you've celebrated the ups and downs of life together, you know when to get out of each other's way, and you know each other's birthdays. These people, in a sense, are extended family, a sort of outer-rim group of people who cover for you when you are sick, who laugh with you when you slip up, who greet you every day over coffee. And now you're leaving? The loss of social capital through retirement is a significant issue. Believe me, your coworkers will probably feel the loss as much as you. They will miss you. Their cards and jokes and hugs are real, and when you first leave, you will be affected by this loss of companionship.

In time, some of those friends will retire too. Others will still be sitting behind the counter, working at the same machine, hovering over

Stump Time!

Some of the people I will miss most are _____.

How can I replace this social capital?_____.

the register. At first, you may have a lot of contact with them, but in time—you know as well as I do—you may drift apart. You will become active with others: groups, organizations, new friends, and old friends who can join you for conversation in your rowboat without the constraints of nine to five.

You have been fortunate to have such good friends at work. No wonder you are leaving some emotional security behind you.

Routine and Predictability

In our house, Joe's routine was constant: up at 6:00 A.M., at work by 7:00 A.M., a half hour lunch (if he bothered to eat lunch), off work at 3:30, home sometime after that. Day in, day out. In the snow and in the rain. Whether he felt well or didn't feel well. For 37 years, Joe Yates' pickup with the familiar JWY license plate was always backed into the same spot at the Swan Lake Ranger District in Bigfork, Montana, ready to go. On the other end, Mrs. Yates would begin to look for that truck to come down the drive around 4:00 P.M.

Unless under a deadline (and therefore not even out of my pajamas), my routine calibrated with Joe's. I'd work until 3:30 or so,

Stump Time!

What part of my routine do I miss? _____.

Should I establish a new routine? _____.

If so, what will it be like? _____.

set the kettle for our afternoon tea, and grow impatient for Wonder Man to come through the door. Nearly every single day we recapped our work over tea. And then an early dinner. It was routine.

You have had a routine for a long time. It was predictable—a little monotonous, yes, but an accustomed comfort as well, like driving down streets you've driven so often it's like shuffling from room to room in a pair of old slippers. You may choose to continue to awaken at the same time each day (that internal clock can be hard to reset!), but any way you look at it, your routine—and its predictability—has been left behind.

Daily Hassles

Don't think I don't know. I've been on the miserable end of a commute. I've ridden the New York City subway, I've been a steady

Stump Time!

The one daily hassle I'm most ready to retire from is ____

_____.

passenger on the Staten Island Ferry, and I've driven over ice-rutted roads in Montana to get to a job 30 miles away. The daily hassle of commuting to work, whether by rail, by ferry, by car, by bus, by bike, or on foot is one thing most of us are happy to leave behind. So is finding a parking space, trying to clean frozen snow off our windshield with a credit card, and cold, wet feet. Not to mention settling for a dry, bland sandwich from the vending machine, coffee that tastes like athletic socks (post-event), and cranky customers or supervisors. Throw in having to iron a shirt or a blouse at the last minute, carpal tunnel syndrome, and a bad back. I'm pretty sure this is one area where we all agree: Sayonara, daily hassles, and good riddance!

The Biggie—Your Legacy

You will leave one more notable thing behind—your legacy. Reputation. You alone have control over how favorable it is.

How are you regarded? How have you left your mark? Will you be thought of with wistful regret that you are no longer there, or with a smirk and a crude comment by coworkers who are just plain glad to see you go? This should matter to you, especially if you claim to follow Jesus Christ—and especially if you've made that

> A man's life is always more forcible than his speech. When men take stock of him they reckon his deeds as dollars and his words as pennies. If his life and doctrine disagree, the mass of onlookers accepts his practice and rejects his preaching.
>
> **Charles Spurgeon**

Stump Time!

What is my legacy? _____.

Did people see Christ in me?_____.

Do people see Christ in me now?_____.

abundantly clear to everyone around you. How much bluster has been attached to your professed faith? Will others think you lived out values worthy of a Christian: trustworthy, kind, productive, speaking no ill of others? Did people see Christ in you? This is your most important legacy and something your coworkers should remember you for.

What You Should Take with You

When the time comes for you to clean out your office, I hope you can take home more than your pictures. I hope that you can take with you a fabulous sense of accomplishment for a job well done. I hope you can look back at how hard you have worked, how you have pressed onward, how you have persevered. I hope you can count coworkers as friends. I hope you have learned skills that you can continue to use to God's glory and for your own good, for the good of your family and your community. I hope that you can take with you a sense of gratitude for the work you had and for its provision. And my greatest hope is that you can take with you a sense of joyful expectation for what lies ahead.

What You Should Go Back For

Go back for that childhood awe. Go back for your dreams.

This is your chance to create a satisfying life, a time (perhaps the first time) to claim some healthy, selfless freedom. You are older and smarter now. I challenge you to reach for the stars. If they seem too high in the sky, string twinkle lights on your bedroom ceiling. It's a start.

And don't worry about money when your head hits the pillow. We'll do that in the next chapter.

4

Financing Retirement
or Retiring Finances?

CYNTHIA:

Thank heavens for government benefits!

By the time I came into Joe's life, his career was well under way, retirement contributions were withheld from his paycheck as a matter of fact, and both of us were what can modestly be called "broke." I was on the slow upswing from financial and emotional devastation as well as a short stint of homelessness with my young son. Joe was under a self-imposed regimen of personal improvement that included weight loss, fiscal responsibility, and avoidance of the popular watering holes in what was once nothing but a wide spot in the road called Bigfork, Montana.

Shortly after our wedding, I suffered the first of many health problems that would eventually decommission me from viable employment and put us deeply into debt—in spite of our health coverage. My escalating medical bills began to choke the life out of Joe's income as we spent untold thousands on deductibles, coinsurance, and alternative therapies that were not covered by insurance. We left no stone unturned as we searched for answers to my persistently poor health. Ten years into our marriage we were dealt a crippling blow when taxes on our tiny lakeside cabin had rocketed from $250 per year to more than $350 per month, sending my husband to our state's capital as a voice begging for fairness in property taxation. His pleas, and the pleas of others, went unheard, and the writing was on the wall for many longtime landowners who had the misfortune (or fortune, depending on perspective) of living in a coveted area of what has come to be called "The Last Best Place." (A river may run through it, but a lot of locals are being swept away on a rising tide as well-heeled people from out of state discover our corner of Montana and want their very own piece.)

Thrifty skills enabled us to cling to our lake property until a bitter day when we faced reality, packed our belongings, and sold our cabin. Yet the beat went on... every two weeks Joe's pay slip announced one true thing: Retirement income, begun so long ago, was in the bank and growing.

Joe:

We were fortunate to have a retirement plan and health insurance, and we were able to sell a house and come away from illnesses and other things pretty much intact. A common expression of mine is "more good luck than good management," but in this case luck had nothing to do with it. It was purely the grace of God. Had it not been for God's grace I would not be here writing this and we would not have been so blessed. I mean that.

Some Words for Those Who Are Retired and Broke

I know you are out there. I know the title of this book caught your eye and you grabbed it hoping for the illusive magic bullet. I know that you scanned through the table of contents to find the finance chapter, and this is the first place you looked. You are not alone.

If you read the first chapter, you know I keep informed by studying reports, statistics, surveys, and the like. What I read has taught me that in spite of any rosy economic predictions (and economic predictions are a mixed bag these days), the average retiree carries a credit card balance of $6000. For many, that debt gets deeper and more dire daily, and as you already know, getting out of debt when you are retired or semiretired is a whole lot harder than when you worked 40 hours a week. That is the main reason you purchased this book: You are in retirement, you are in debt, and you need help. I understand, and I want to start this chapter with assurance.

I have encountered countless people who fret over their financial security in later life, some having more to worry about than others. Throughout the process of writing this book, I have had cash-strapped retirees practically coming out of the woodwork and baring their souls to me. It usually starts like this:

"What's your next book about, Cynthia?"

"Living well in retirement."

(Long pause.) "I could use a book like that."

I once met a dear, older woman whom I will call Mabel. Mabel was at a women's retreat I was giving on frugal living. During the closing hour of the retreat, I challenged the women in the room to write one word that described their emotional response to their financial situation. Around the room we went: angry, sad, comfortable, pretty good, guilty...and then we came to Mabel.

Mabel was one of the church leaders. Her history with that congregation was long, mutually beneficial, and distinguished. She presented herself in a dignified manner, dressed impeccably, and appeared to have it all together. We could look at Mabel and think to ourselves, *She definitely lives well.*

> Credit card accounts are designed to keep you in debt. If you want to go into retirement with an iota of financial stability and security, control your consumer debt.

> Which of you, if his son asks for bread, will give him a stone? Or if he asks for a fish, will give him a snake? If you, then, though you are evil, know how to give good gifts to your children, how much more will your Father in heaven give good gifts to those who ask him!
>
> Matthew 7:9-11

Mabel began to cry. Mabel's word was *scared*.

Every woman's head whipped to attention as if they were all attached by a puppeteer's cord. A shocked silence—positively pregnant with concern—settled over the room as Mabel spoke.

"We can't make ends meet. I got a credit card in the mail, so I went to the bank every month and took a cash advance. Now I don't know how we are going to pay it back. They are starting to call me at home because I was late with the payment once. That bumped my interest rate up to 25 percent. I don't know what to do."

I am happy to tell you that Mabel's church got behind her, and with their help and a few new skills, she and her husband are once again solvent—though their lifestyle took a few hits.

You May Be Scared Too

I can't wave a magic wand, send the Prize Patrol to your door with balloons and flowers, or put money under your pillow while you sleep, but I can help.

Again and again I'm going to insist that you approach every hurdle holistically: body, mind, spirit. This is *particularly* true if you are financially strapped.

Prayer should be your first recourse. Pray for forgiveness if you've squandered money. Pray for guidance and wise counsel if you don't know where to turn. Pray for a miracle.

Funny how this works, but God usually has to use some big upset in our lives to get our attention. Rest assured, at issue is not how long you took to acknowledge Him, but that you did. Prayer should be your first recourse in everything.

And then there are your utterly crushed feelings over your situation. I've talked about attitude already, but consider how important a positive, can-do attitude is right now.

Or a no-can-do-attitude. Here's what I mean.

Some already-retired seniors are old enough to have felt the lingering effect of our Great Depression, and the primary effect was learning how to be frugal. You reuse your dental floss, stoop to pick pennies off the ground, use one teabag to a pot (doesn't everybody?), never, *ever* throw food in the garbage, and drive a trusty older car, which you probably paid for with cash. You have always been able to get by and to make do, and you sacrificed plenty to do so.

Along with your frugal training came a sense of self-reliance, a self-sufficiency that has carried you through life and carried you well. *I can do it myself, take care of it myself, pay for it myself, fix it myself,* ad infinitum. So guess what comes hand in hand with such confidence and proficiency? Yup—pride. The right kind of pride is good. Most pride isn't.

Pride can be harmful to your financial life. This is the "bite off my nose to spite my face" kind of pride, and one variation is a bullheaded determination to "go without" before asking for help—especially from family members, and *most* especially from adult children, and *certainly* from the government. Why, that would be welfare. Besides, what kind of phony or failure would you be in everyone's eyes if you—the very one who has promoted savings and restraint— were in a financial pickle barrel?

> **W**hen pride comes, then comes disgrace, but with humility comes wisdom.
> **Proverbs 11:2**

Oh, please! As I've already written, life happens. Medical bills happen. The rising cost of living happens. Your body getting too old and feeble to do what it once did so you pay a fortune to others to do yard work or home maintenance happens. Being utterly lost in a world that has changed radically happens. Just like Mabel and her husband, not being able to keep up happens. And it happens more than we think.

Good people end up in debt. All the enthusiasm and determination in the world isn't going to stop the bill collector from closing in. If your confidence is as maxed as your credit line and you are horrified at the prospect of bankruptcy, help is available. Consumer Credit Counseling Services is a nonprofit organization with hundreds of offices nationwide. Look in your Yellow Pages for the number of an office near you. These people might be able to help. Many churches have members who volunteer their services and can guide you through these troubled waters.

But beware! Some credit clinics charge exorbitant rates for their services and get away with it because people are desperate. Be exceedingly careful with whom you do business.

You can sometimes get help from the very people who are hired to wring that last dime from your checking account. Collection agencies will often work with you if you demonstrate a willing spirit. Communicate. You may be able to work out a solution with them.

Bankruptcy

What if your credit is kaput and you have no way out of that pickle barrel? Bankruptcy may be your last resort, but it contains long-term negative consequences that can affect all aspects of your life for years to come.

Should you declare bankruptcy? Is it a responsible thing to do? Good question. It may be time for a reminder that how we handle everything in life—including debt—reflects on Jesus. This is no small thing. You may have to consider bankruptcy if you have no other options, if the opinion of trusted professionals is that this is necessary, and if you will try to repay your debt when you are solvent.

In any case, bankruptcy does not discharge you from all debt. Some obligations cannot be eliminated by filing bankruptcy, including these:

- taxes due the IRS
- alimony and child support
- guaranteed student loans

- liabilities created by fraudulent action
- liabilities resulting from theft or destruction of private property
- debt not reported on bankruptcy forms, or debts for which the creditor's name and address were incorrectly listed

Bankruptcy stays on your credit record for ten years. Agencies such as Consumer Credit Counseling Service will advise you on what steps to take to bring vibrancy and health back to your creditworthiness. The important thing for you to remember is that other people have walked in your shoes. Many of those people are smiling now.

> I have an important message for your book. Tell your readers that no matter how well they think they have planned it, it's not what they perceive. They have to be flexible both financially and psychologically.
>
> **Wonder Man**

Harvard's *Consumer Bankruptcy Project* recently concluded that seniors filing for bankruptcy are the fastest growing group of petitioners. One expert claims the reason for this is the "weakening of the three-legged stool": Social Security, pensions, and private savings.

(I'm reminded of my maternal grandmother, who "got along" on Social Security for many years until her death at 78. Let me tell you what that meant: She lived with us. My mother "gets along" on Social Security and a small pension from her service at General Electric. Let me tell you what that means: She lives with my sister. Defying all statistics, my mom is still going strong at 89.)

If it's not too late, shore up that stool by adding a few extra legs. If you are able, evaluate your financial predicament and then seek help. (If you are not up to this, seek help from a family member, a friend, or an advocacy group.) As much as some of you may hate to consider this, government aid is available, including Medicaid, housing, supplemental income, and food stamps.

An adult child is the first place to turn for help. Lest you feel sheepish, may I remind you of the time, money, and love you have poured into that kid? Or of the biblical imperative found in Proverbs 23:22?

> Hearken unto thy father that begat thee, and despise not thy mother when she is old (KJV).

> Listen to your father, who gave you life, and do not despise your mother when she is old.

> Listen with respect to the father who raised you, and when your mother grows old, don't neglect her (MSG).

For those of you who could use a little help to either hone skills or to learn frugal skills, my last two books might prove helpful: *Living Well on One Income* and *Ditch the Diet and the Budget...and Find a Better Way to Live* (Harvest House).

> If you cosign for anyone (like your kids), be doubly and triply sure guaranteed notification is built in should any payments become overdue.

Other options include trying to find other sources of income. Can you sell something in your home? Could you have a yard sale? Can you work part-time for a seasonal event or at a seasonal business?

If you have found yourselves on the threshold of retirement with no planned income in sight, read on.

The Perfect Plan

Yes, I know. The perfect plan for you right now is one that will provide a terrific retirement income in record time. Like overnight. Sorry.

For retirement you will need both short-term and long-term strategies, and goal setting should never end. The perfect financial preretirement plan is one that is tailor-made to your circumstance, your goals, your personality, your health, and your determination to succeed. It must have flexibility as well as safety checks built in. Flexibility is necessary because, as I have written, life happens. A safety check is necessary because temptation happens. Oh, I forgot—temptation doesn't happen to *you*...

The quickest way to double your money is to fold it in half and put it back in your pocket.

- Man, I want that boat so *badly.*

- Wow! I've never run across such an investment opportunity before—a gold mine in the Yucatan! My brother-in-law says it's a sure bet.

- I've never said no to my son before—he wouldn't ask if he didn't need the money.

- What would it hurt if I tapped into my savings just a little?

All of us already have a plan—did you know that? You may be planning by not having a plan: planning to work until the day you die, planning to stay perfectly healthy and strong so you can work until the day you die, planning for your husband or wife to stay perfectly healthy and work until the day he or she dies. You may also be "planning" to live in near-poverty conditions or to face years of anxiety and anguish over how you are going to pay the bills.

Some plan.

Go to the Pro

Learning when and how to allocate your money during retirement is utterly essential. Where can you find the help you need to negotiate the twists and turns of retirement planning? If I had my way, you'd go to a pro. (One pro, a fellow named Jack North, feels that the most critical asset you can invest into your retirement plan is time. Take the time to plan, evaluate, and manage your retirement investments.) In my experience, the professional planner's fee is money well spent if you are utterly out of your area of expertise. Usually, professionals *save* us money overall, especially in murky areas that include taxes, because most people are utterly at sea when it comes to disbursing retirement funds.

Some of you already have financial gurus guiding your every nickel and dime. These are people who are trained and qualified to counsel you regarding investments, taxes, and your estate. (Taxation can play a huge role in retirement income, so plan wisely!) If you can, I urge you to enlist the aid of a *seasoned* professional. No offense to your earnest nephew who just landed a job with Investyourmoneyhere. This is your money. It is also your future security. An experienced professional should be your choice for counsel. Your best choice may be to hire a financial planner who is fee-based rather than someone who charges a percentage of your portfolio. Regardless of your advisor's fee structure, be vigilant to every single cost associated with your retirement portfolio, including tax liability, commissions, and fees.

Above all, you want a professional who has a reputation for honesty, who is easy to understand, and who communicates regularly.

Also, as was our case, many employers provide the assistance of retirement experts who offer seminars to those approaching retirement age. Workshops, complete with sample exercises and formulas, can be extremely helpful.

Beth Morgenstern is an investment representative with Edward Jones. She graciously agreed to review this chapter for accuracy. How did I find a local woman with up-to-the-minute expertise in all areas of financial planning? I read her newspaper ad announcing an estate and retirement planning seminar. And then I interviewed her.

(Beth informs me that her firm has an excellent retirement calculation system and that any office nationwide would be happy to help.)

Asking the human resources department from your firm to do a mock run of your retirement benefits is also helpful, as is contacting Social Security for probable benefits should you retire.

Community colleges, universities, senior advocacy groups, magazines, and other publications offer many levels of assistance. Many such organizations, books, and periodicals are listed in the back of this book.

A few words from Beth:

You may think you are retired, but you are now a chief financial officer! It is your duty to manage your finances to provide the lifestyle you desire.

Interview advisors carefully. Professionals and firms have different philosophies. Hire someone you are comfortable with, who communicates well. Your advisor should encourage you to ask questions and should be available readily. If you are unhappy with your advisor, find a new one. It's your money, and it deserves top-quality attention.

You owe it to yourself to understand your assets. Get educated so that you can make smart financial decisions.

How Much Do You Need?

To plan for retirement, you must know how much you need to save in order to retire with the income you will need. A simple rule of thumb: For every $1000 needed in monthly income, you need a savings of $250,000 earning between 4 and 5 percent interest. With one of the free online retirement payout calculators, you can plan more precisely using your own investment amount, rate of return, and length of retirement.

(This is one time when a carton of rocky road ice cream and a spoon are perfectly permissible. You may need a carbohydrate fix right now to get over your shock. I'll wait.)

Conventional wisdom (whatever that is) says you will need as little as 70 percent of your preretirement income for retirement, and I've also read that you'll need as much as 85 percent. Joe and I were coached to have 80 percent.

More and more planners are insisting that you need 100 percent (or more) of your preretirement income for retirement. They back their claims by pointing to other countries that are beginning to abandon such percentage-based retirement formulas. So much for conventional wisdom.

From One Woman to Another

"Tell other women to learn from me. Look at me. I could have saved, but I didn't. Now it's too late. I'm stuck in low-income housing and have to depend on my kids to pay for any extras."

The smartest thing a woman can do to protect herself financially is to start saving for retirement. You can't start too soon, and it's only going to get more expensive to maintain your lifestyle.

From One Man to Another

"You read the papers and get the impression that everyone's declaring bankruptcy, and it's a piece of cake. Well, take it from me, it isn't. We have suffered over and over again because of our bankruptcy. Like right now, we really need a new car, but we can't get credit."

Most people deal with their finances on an event-by-event basis. That is after-the-fact planning.

In a perfect world, your mortgage and other significant bills will be "retired" by the time you are, freeing money that will bring your level of expendable income to par with preretirement status or higher.

Can You Afford to Retire?

I've read that fewer than 5 percent of all U.S. families will be able to match their current standard of living in retirement without additional employment. Even if we bump that figure up to fewer than 10 percent, that still leaves 90 percent of us—or 9 out of 10 retirees—who will be adjusting their lifestyle downward to match their retirement income. This isn't the end of the world. It is a fact that a high percentage of people will retire to a lower standard of living. So what? I'm not trying to be flippant, but flip this conundrum inside out and call it something else. Rather than a lower standard of living, let's call it a *different* standard of living. Change is upon you. Might as well embrace it.

A different standard of living is not the end of life as you know it. You do have options:

- A full-blown second career. (Not retirement at all, but a paradigm shift.)

- Part-time work. (This doubles as both a financial boost and an esteem enhancement.)

- Minimal, moderate, or radical change in lifestyle. (It's time for a change anyway.)

- Live in a tent on a beach someplace. (Don't laugh, I know people who did this in Mexico and loved it!)

- Live in shared housing with other retirees. (A new phenomenon within adult circles that is gaining popularity—a "retirement commune." Maybe because so many of us were hippies once upon a time.)

- Live with the kids. (So what if you have to share the bathroom with the grandkids?)

Dude, You Need a Budget

You can only determine whether you can afford to retire if you use the "B" word. Whether you are already retired or tossing the notion around, you need a retirement budget. A budget is nothing more or less than a plan of what you will spend. Once you know how much you will spend, you need to know where the money is coming from. Here are some questions to consider before you begin to determine your monetary needs:

- Will the mortgage be paid?

- Will all the children be out of the home and on their own?

- Do I anticipate extra expenses, such as caring for an elderly parent or a special needs adult child?

- Will costly loans be paid?

- How is my health and the health of my spouse?

- How much does it cost to live now?

- Do I plan to maintain my home as well as my current standard of living?

- Do I plan to travel or to participate in a costly sport or pastime?

Use the following worksheet to determine your monthly expenses in retirement.

Expense items	Monthly amount
Giving	
tithe, pledges, charitable gifts.	_____
Savings and life insurance.	_____
Housing	
principal, interest, insurance, taxes (or rent).	_____
maintenance and repairs	_____
utilities (gas, electricity, water, garbage).	_____
furniture and housewares	_____
Transportation	
car payments	_____
gas.	_____
maintenance and repairs	_____
licenses and registrations	_____
auto insurance	_____
Groceries and restaurants	_____
Clothing	_____
Medical and dental	
insurance premiums	_____
co-pays for appointments and medications.	_____
over-the-counter medications.	_____
long-term care	_____
Loan and debt reduction payments.	_____

Telephone and cell phone . . . . _____

Internet provider and cable. . . . . _____

Pet care . . . . _____

Recreation and entertainment. . . . . _____

Alimony and child support. . . . . _____

Gifts . . . . _____

Magazine subscriptions and books . . . . _____

Annual dues . . . . _____

Personal items. . . . . _____

Other. . . . . _____

Total . . . . _____

Once you tally your projected monthly expenses, add up to 25 percent to compensate for inflation and new costs that are bound to come your way, such as higher insurance premiums and medical bills. Once you determine your projected monthly costs, try to extend that cost into years you hope to live. As mentioned in chapter 1, statistics show that men now live to age 80, women to age 84.

My projected monthly expense is $ _____.

That makes my projected yearly cost of living $ _____.

If I live _____ more years, I would need at least $ _____ to cover these expenses.

Now you have to figure out where the money is coming from. Determine the rate of return from your investments and other sources of income. (It is wise to also evaluate your need for access to your principal, and how accessible that principal is.)

Income-Producing Assets	Value	Projected Monthly Income
Pension/retirement plans	_____	_____
Social Security	_____	_____
Rental property	_____	_____
Insurance policies/ annuities	_____	_____
Trust income	_____	_____

Income-Producing Assets	Value	Projected Monthly Income
Stocks and mutual funds	_____	_____
Bonds	_____	_____
Alimony	_____	_____
Savings and CDs	_____	_____
Other	_____	_____
Total	_____	_____

Now the rubber meets the road: Compare your monthly retirement income against your monthly expenditures, and you will know if you can afford to retire, providing you wish to maintain status quo.

In order to live comfortably, I need $ _____ each month during my retirement years.

Based on various sources, I project $ _____ each month in income.

The difference is $ _____ plus/minus.

Two Caveats

I am both a realist and a romantic. (Which makes me romantically real or really romantic.) Take your pick, but at the end of the day, reality trumps romanticism. I may dance under the stars with gusto, but one of my feet is always planted firmly on the ground. Because of that I want to get real with you right now about the two "aces in the hole" many of us seem to be depending upon.

I can hear many of you now:

1. *I plan to get a part-time job to supplement our retirement income.* (Joe daydreamed a bit about becoming the paint guy at one of those home improvement stores—that has *got* to be a man thing!)

2. *I'm living in my retirement. I plan to sell the house, make a bundle, and move someplace less expensive.*

To both of those sentiments I say, more power to you! Go for it! Been done thousands of times before! And watch out! Here's what I mean:

The Part-Time Job

Did you read the statistics in chapter 1? Between 76 and 79 *million* boomers will be retiring over the next several years. How many greeters do you think a place like Wal-Mart can hire?

If you plan to get another job, begin to lay the groundwork *now*. Establish contacts, start writing a résumé, and get training. Be proactive. A squeaky wheel does get greased and persistence does pay. Do not depend on this additional income until it is certain. Stories abound of people from all walks of life, from every conceivable academic and educational background, who search for work to no avail. In my husband's case, through diligence and foresight, he was able to find part-time retirement work that remarkably suited his skills and personality, and he worked hard before retirement to "line up his ducks."

The House Sale

How well I remember the moment years ago when Joe and I were standing on the deck of our cabin looking down on Flathead Lake near Bigfork, Montana. "I plan to sell this place to finance retirement," he announced in a cool, matter-of-fact tone, instantly losing his Wonder Man status. I could have dropped stone dead. Really. How could he *think* of such a thing? This was our refuge, our sanctuary, our cabin on the lake! I expected our grandkids to grow up there, in that very spot. Frantic, I went into overdrive to convince him otherwise. Little did we both know his words would one day ring true, not to finance retirement, but to buy our way out of debt.

Let's go back to the stats: 76 to 79 *million*. Of that, statistically, somewhere between 40 to 50 percent of retirees intend to sell and relocate. Okeydokey…

So all these houses are suddenly going to hit the market—at a time when demographics will be shifting and fewer young workers with purchasing power will be available to buy them. (The two-children-max per family craze and abortion are but two factors in this coming phenomenon.)

A little factoid before I ask you to consider some questions: In 2001, the median value of homes owned by older persons was $107,398, compared to a median home value of $123,889 for all homeowners. About 73 percent of older homeowners in 2001 owned their homes free and clear.[1] And now the questions:

- Will the real estate boom of recent years remain viable? Some forecasters say yes, it will…but the boom remains regional and site-specific. The real estate magazine in our neck of the woods looks at times like the New York City phone book.

- Will interest rates stay historically low?

- Will your house pass muster: its curb appeal (including an attractive neighborhood), its inside sales appeal, the inspection, and the appraisal?

- Will some neighbor open a Harley repair shop two doors down before you sell?

Lots of people have sold at a profit and you may too. But ignoring the potential for disappointment would be imprudent. While I am at it, I'd like to expand on this house issue.

Unless you have sound advice and are dealing with a sure thing, if you are of retirement age, I beg you to reconsider before you refinance your house in order to obtain cash flow. I fear that many of us have already made this risky transaction, only to face a mortgage payment far into retirement years. (Banking on the future sale of your house to pay off the mortgage may *force* you to sell your house.) A whole lot of us are living in the only equity we can claim: our home. Once it is gone, it is gone. Do not do anything rash when you contemplate the wise use of this equity. Also consider the tax advantages that you may now enjoy as a result of home ownership.

On the other hand, you must factor in the cost of living in your house. If maintaining your house is costing you a bundle, by all means, downsize. If you are facing a radical change in your lifestyle or if your situation is grim, this may be the first thing to go. It's okay—you'll have fun scaling down and decorating your new place. (Chapter 9 addresses the issue of where to live.)

Retirement Income: A Primer

Social Security

Social Security provides monthly payments to qualified workers who retire at age 62 or older, Medicare coverage for the elderly, and disability payments. It also provides spousal benefits and benefits to children.

The fervent hope of many of us boomers is that Social Security will last at least as long as we do—in one form or another. Yet even if it does manage to stay afloat, Social Security doesn't promise a lot. It should be considered as *part* of your retirement income. The government has already raised eligibility to 67 for those born after 1960, and the government can change the benefit age again. As this book was in the writing, I heard Alan Greenspan urgently insist that Social Security benefits be reduced—and fast. Why? The boomer generation was nipping at the door.

Once you are collecting Social Security, the benefits may be decreased if you earn extra income before age 65. The way it stands now, if you are age 65 or older you may earn any additional income without penalty to benefits. If you are younger than age 65, you may earn up to $10,680 annually without penalty to benefits. Any income over $10,680 deducts $1 from your benefit for every $2 above that limit. If you postpone benefits until age 70, you may get a credit benefit for delaying retirement.

Incidentally, widows do not automatically lose their deceased husband's Social Security benefits if they remarry *after age 60*. They have three options:

1. keep their deceased spouse's benefits
2. receive a percentage of their new spouse's benefits
3. keep their own benefits

Employee Retirement Plans

Are you in a vested retirement plan at work? The law requires your employer to provide you with a projection of estimated retirement income if you ask for one. "Vested" means that you have secured the right of possession. Find out what kind of plan your employer participates in, how reliable it is, what the history of the plan is, how it is backed, and what types of options you have. This is your money. One advisor insists that you obtain a fee breakdown from your benefits department and that you should complain in writing if you are paying more than 1 percent for a bond fund, 1.25 percent for a domestic stock fund, or 1.5 percent for an international stock fund.

Qualified pension plans have lost some popularity through the years, partly because of a corporation's minimum funding requirement and harsh financial consequences if the plan is under funded. Many corporations are turning to deferred profit sharing plans such as a 401(k) for employee retirement benefits. Under a deferred profit sharing plan, a specified percentage (with no guarantees of specific amounts) of company profits is invested into a qualified profit sharing plan. This is different from a qualified pension plan, which is subject to investment amounts called for by the plan itself.

> **N**amed beneficiaries on retirement plans supercede those on a will.

A "defined benefit" plan provides a monthly payment in retirement that is based on length of service and earnings and does not usually protect against inflation.

A "defined contribution" plan such as a 401(k) provides a monthly payment in retirement that is based on your investment. This is sometimes accomplished through an annuity once the fund is rolled over. A good advisor is plenty helpful at this point.

Pension Rights

The Employer Retirement Income Security Act (ERISA) was hatched by Congress to protect pension assets. It is a federal law designed to ensure that money you put in private employee retirement plans will be there when you retire. The law ensures you must be provided a Summary Plan Description when asked. This is very important to you.

The SPD gives you all the details about your plan, including what it provides, how it works, how benefits are calculated, your contribution, when you are vested, and how to apply for the benefits. ERISA also requires your pension provider to provide a copy of the plan's summary annual report.

Most pension plans must file a summary annual report (Form 5500) with the U.S. Department of Labor. If you have any difficulties with your pension administrator and are unsuccessful in your requests for information, contact the Employee Benefits Security Administration at the Department of Labor. You can reach them online at www.askebsa.dol.gov.

ERISA also created the Pension Benefit Guaranty Corporation, which is a federal agency designed to protect all defined benefit pensions. It does not protect a deferred contribution plan such as a 401(k). Your summary plan description will let you know if your plan is protected by the PBGC.

Spousal Rights

If your spouse wishes to reject survivor benefits on your pension payment, he or she has to agree to this option in writing. Spousal rights to benefits is a critical issue, so get professional advice!

Extra Help with Pensions

The Pension Rights Center is a consumer organization that advocates for American workers, retirees, and families. This group offers critical services through their counseling projects, their educational material, and their advocacy. They are based in Washington, D.C. The Web address is www.pensionrights.org.

Individual Retirement Accounts (IRAs)

This is a common retirement account for working and nonworking spouses of workers. It allows you to invest or save up to a certain amount each year and to deduct it from your tax return. You can invest through a bank, through an investment firm, through mutual funds, or even through other intangible investments, such as stocks. Banks often compete for IRA funds and may offer appealing guaranteed interest rates. Mutual funds, on the other hand, tend to offer greater payoff but have some risk as well.

The immediate benefit of an IRA account is the investing of your pretax dollar, thereby reducing your taxable income. You will pay a penalty and tax if you withdraw IRA funds before age 59 and a half, and you will pay tax on any withdrawals after that time. Penalties for early withdrawal can be waived under certain circumstances, such as severe medical expense, tuition for college, or primary home purchase for yourself or your children.

If you let your money sit in the IRA account after you are 70 and a half, the IRS will begin to penalize you, and the penalty is nasty: As much as 50 percent of the amount of your minimum distribution can be demanded as tax. Changes in the tax code and in the rules governing IRAs are regular. Check with a professional to stay up-to-date.

Incidentally, all funds left in a traditional IRA go to heirs at the time of death, and they pay tax based on their tax bracket.

Tax Time Bomb

Some financial consultants refer to any tax-deferred investments as tax time bombs. They have a point. Many of us have invested in pensions and IRAs, expecting that two things will be to our benefit when we retire: (1) We will be in a much lower tax bracket, due to reduced income, and therefore the tax penalty on withdrawing from our tax-deferred funds will be lessened; and (2) government regulations on taxes will not change to our detriment by the time we retire.

Some experts recommend minimizing your tax penalty now rather than facing uncertain tax laws in the future. Their position is in contrast to conventional wisdom, which encourages you to invest pretax dollars now and take your lumps later. You should use a common-sense approach to all of your investments and consider both sides of the coin. Neither you nor your representative should do anything with your assets without first considering tax consequence.

Roth IRAs

Many financial consultants feel a Roth IRA is the best option for savings. This is an IRA that is funded with after-tax dollars, thereby allowing you tax-free withdrawals. The principal accrues tax free. A Roth IRA should be considered on an individual basis. Some people convert their traditional IRA to a Roth, even though they have to pay taxes on the converted amount. Stop by your bank or broker and grab an explanatory brochure on the merits of a Roth IRA. For some, this is an attractive deal. This investment opportunity seems like a compromise between those who counsel you to take your lumps now and those who promote tax-deferred investments.

Simplified Employee Pension (SEP IRAs)

If you are self-employed, you may invest up to 25 percent of your self-employed income into a SEP IRA. (If you have employees, you may have to make a like contribution for each employee at the same rate.) If you retrieve your funds before age 59 and a half, you will be subject to penalty unless you've established a lifetime distribution program. Also, you will be penalized if you don't begin to withdraw funds by age 70 and a half. Again, a good advisor will navigate you through these waters.

401(k) and 403(b)

This plan is defined by the employer and provides for pretax investment by the employee. The employer may choose to contribute a fixed amount to the employee's plan or match the employee's contribution. The money in a 401(k) can be invested in a diversity of places, which run the gamut from conservative to risky. A 401(k) has a higher ceiling of pretax dollars than an IRA. Many financial experts counsel clients to invest in an IRA each year as well as a 401(k). If husband and wife each participate in a 401(k), they should consider managing the plans together and giving priority to the plan with the greater employer contributions.

A 403(b) is a similar plan for nonprofit groups and is less likely than a 401(k) to have employer matching funds.

Annuities

An annuity is a contract with an insurance company in which a certain amount of money is invested in exchange for a certain income for yourself (or loved one) for a certain time. Here's how it works: Suppose you just turned 50, and you've scratched some figures on a pad to come up with how much you will need at retirement. You could then invest in an annuity either by paying a lump sum or by paying a lump sum followed by additional payments into the annuity.

When you retire, the annuity will begin to pay. Annuities can be custom-made to pay in a lump sum, monthly allotments, lifetime allotments, or payments to a beneficiary if you die. The interest you earn on the annuity is tax-deferred. As with other retirement plans, the idea is that when you retire you will be in a lower tax bracket and will pay less tax on the income from the annuity. In that regard, annuities are touted as a method to defer taxes. Remember that this assumption may prove false. Furthermore, when you purchase an annuity, your money is not available before maturity without paying a penalty. Also, a woman's annuity payments are less because women tend to live longer.

A "variable" annuity invests part of your investment into mutual funds. This method offers potentially greater growth but more risk.

A gradually funded annuity allows the purchase of immediate annuities over several years, in turn allowing for better interest rates in the future, which in turn will allow for higher payments.

Life Insurance

As someone who was once a vigorous supporter of life insurance as an investment (as someone who once *taught* life insurance), I must recant. Cash value on a policy is often considered a poor rate of return for your dollar. I still do believe everyone should have some amount of permanent insurance, preferably purchased at such a young age that the premiums are negligible. One reason I emphasize this is to protect the insurability of the person. I do, however, support the need to buy term insurance, which can be viewed as supplemental insurance that you "rent" when your need for high amounts of insurance is great, such as during vulnerable years or when you have family or business responsibility. Unlike permanent insurance, which accrues a cash value, term insurance (which is significantly less expensive) merely provides a death benefit.

Should you have life insurance? Well, shoot—at least enough to bury you, don't you think? Will your heirs need a substantial amount of money for their care (perhaps long-term care)? How much does it cost to maintain life insurance coverage? Can your existing coverage be reduced?

(I recently tried to reduce the $100,000 term policy on my life to $50,000 but was told the policy held a $100,000 minimum. I've had this policy for a long time and plan to keep it [especially with my health history] until I feel certain that Joe is rock-solid secure should I die. Besides, I might like to leave the grandkids a little "kicker.")

This question of life insurance is one reason why I recommend you seek a financial advisor.

Other Income

In addition to a formal retirement investment (or in lieu of one), you may receive trust income, rental income, royalties, and income from your investments in bonds, the stock market, and mutual funds.

It makes good sense for you to have a little cushion on hand when you actually retire—a few months' "walking around money," as Joe would call it.

The reason is valid: Suppose you have a solid retirement portfolio but need to start collecting at exactly the same time that interest rates are low or the country is experiencing a bear market (a down market)? You need liq-

Death and taxes will always be with us, but death doesn't get worse every year.

uidity to get you through a "bear" of a time. If you have the lead time and the money to put aside, take out a certificate of deposit that will mature when you retire, or keep some money stashed in a money market account.

Get Thee Some Tax Knowledge

Tax savvy and tax planning are essential when considering retirement income. You can't list the cocker spaniel as an exemption, but you sure can legally and righteously list deductions that will lessen your tax load, and you can shelter some income from taxation.

For instance, are you aware that your Social Security benefits are taxable if you exceed a certain annual income? Or that geography plays a big role in taxation? Many states do not tax income from Social Security, some states treat retirement benefits differently than they do other income, and some states (such as Montana) are particularly hard on retirement income.

Tax penalties exist for transferring a family business, for having too many tax shelters, and for retiring to another state. Oh, brudder! Go *die* in another state, and you may create a tax trap for your heirs!

Some people who retire may be so accustomed to having their withholding automatically deducted by their employers that they will be blindsided by a whopping tax bill when April 15 rolls around.

A Word About Your Estate

Some people do not consider making a plan for what happens to their estate when they die. But without some kind of plan, you could inadvertently disinherit loved ones and create havoc in the lives of those left behind. An estate plan is an act of love.

An estate plan is a highly personal review and plan to protect or pass along your estate. Your estate is the sum total of your tangible and intangible assets and liabilities at the time of your death. An estate plan can also preserve your standard of living and your capital assets while you are alive.

Often mistakenly believed to be reserved for the well-to-do, an estate plan is a formal (and often legal) document that spells out how you want your estate distributed to rightful heirs. It can also protect heirs (and minor children) in the event of your death. This sounds like a will, doesn't it? There is a difference.

Call the estate plan your mission statement: a comprehensive consideration of all aspects of estate transfer to designated beneficiaries.

Your will becomes part of your specific plan—it specifies who will receive what and designates an administrator (an executor).

A good estate plan will include more:

- The care and rearing of children and dependents.

- Taxes, which are a huge consideration with some estates. Many tax traps can swallow personal estates whole, and they could have been avoided under the counsel and guidance of an experienced estate planner.

- Personal wishes regarding the distribution of assets, the liquidation of the estate, and the care of a surviving spouse.

- How to pay debts. An estate plan should provide enough liquid funds to pay immediate debts. Debts against the estate must be brought to some kind of resolution when the property holder dies. Unless proper plans have been laid, in some states, bank accounts can be frozen and safe deposit boxes sealed.

- Your estate plan should also include documents with provisions that will meet your needs should you need care during your lifetime.

A Will

A will expresses your wishes for the distribution of what you leave behind. If you die intestate (without a will), the probate laws of your state kick in. That means an impersonal judge will make the decisions *you* should have made: who gets your kids, what portion of your estate will go to your spouse, who gets the house and the car, and whether your second cousin twice removed (the one you really, really don't like) gets a piece of your estate pie. Incidentally, state laws vary as to the percentage of the estate the surviving spouse should receive. And in some states, children are entitled to a certain percentage, regardless of the provisions in the will.

If you die without a will, you will leave an unfair burden upon your heirs, who now have to go through a legal and sometimes expensive rigmarole to access your estate.

Stump Time!

1. ❏ Yes ❏ No   I'm prepared, so I can laugh at the days to come.

2. ❏ Yes ❏ No   I don't care about the future.

3. ❏ Yes ❏ No   I will never, ever get sick.

4. ❏ Yes ❏ No   My spouse will always be there for me.

5. ❏ Yes ❏ No   My children will always be there for me.

6. ❏ Yes ❏ No   My dog will always be there for me.

7. ❏ Yes ❏ No   Saving money for any reason is impossible for me.

8. ❏ Yes ❏ No   I'd rather spend money on things I want now.

9. ❏ Yes ❏ No   Jesus is coming, so I don't have to worry about retirement.

10. ❏ Yes ❏ No   I think saving something for the future is a good idea.

5

In Sickness
and in Retirement

CYNTHIA:

Getting back to that fateful cross-country drive after Joe retired...

I think what made matters worse for me as Joe and I hurtled east toward Virginia was that I was on record telling everyone what a super marriage we had. I'm not talking about telling friends over tea—I'm talking about telling, you know, *the whole world* through TV, radio, books, magazines, and inspirational talks. *That* kind of telling.

I had shared our story with millions: how we'd overcome just about every adversity this side of adultery, how we were at the top of our game. In love, devoted, dedicated—that was us. Hah! My emotions smoldered while "Wonder Man" simmered just under a boil. You may find this hard to believe, but I would have turned the car around and headed back toward Montana if I hadn't calculated the cost. True to my frugal nature, the adding machine in my brain started adding and subtracting:

Nope, we've spent too much money already. We're halfway there, and can't go back. Fine…let him stew.

It's not a stretch to say my pride was as damaged as my brain was addled. I could not understand how discord could blindside us with such force. And make us mad as hornets. Us! Mad! It was all too wrong, too baffling.

The fact that our marriage could derail so easily, so effortlessly, left me shaken. Sure, we'd had trouble in the past, but this…this was like some weird nightmare.

JOE:

Well, let's get another perspective: I'm retired, right? Cynthia's plan is that four days later I'll be on the other side of the country. Remember, I'm just retired! We had guests staying with us for the retirement party and when they left, so did we. Twenty-three hundred miles in three and a half days. Soon we will be at our son's house to relax and care for our two grandchildren (ages four and less than one) with all six of us living in one house. And then I think, "Re" and "tired"…that sounds to me like "tired again." Well, I haven't even rested to be re-tired!

A number of other issues were also affecting our swan song retirement trip. What happens if the calculations on the retirement check aren't right? Do I need to stop at Wal-Mart, Costco, Kmart, or Scrub Yer Car and get a job?

We'd had a long three years of being apart. Cynthia's in Montana, I'm away on a work detail. I'm in Montana, Cynthia's at the kids. Cynthia's home, I'm gone on a fire or working 14-hour days during planting season. Life as we once knew it—us—had become a faint memory, and traveling at Mach 1 across the country and moving in with four others, there wasn't a moment for us.

Close Relations

You have a relationship with *some*body.

You may live in the tundra of Alaska and get your groceries by sea-plane, but you know and relate to *some*one, if only the pilot. Even the Lone Ranger had Tonto. (When our son was young, he referred to this fellow as the Strange Ranger with his sidekick Toronto.) The subject of others—for what is living well if not living well with others—will be addressed later. This chapter is dedicated to the one relationship that is affected by retirement as no other: marriage.

How many times I've heard women rant and complain about their husbands after they had retired! I secretly scoffed at those women and judged them shallow, their love provisional, their minds weak or closed. But since Joe's retirement, I've sometimes rued my self-righteous judgment of those women.

Shall We Dance?

As I've made clear through our story, retirement affects both part-ners in a marriage, whether one continues to work or not. We are thrown off balance. Some of us are nimble on our feet and are able to adjust quickly. Some of us are lummoxes.

Marriage is like a dance. Actually, it is like several dances. You learn the steps, stub your toes, and eventually figure out where to place your feet when you hear the beat. By the time you face retirement, chances are you've danced together a long, long time. And then—suddenly—you are hearing a totally new rhythm, a different beat, and you are nothing but feet. Or you suddenly fancy yourself the leader of the band and cannot for the life of you understand why your mate has turned into a wallflower.

Hold on. Be patient. Both of you.

Variations of the Retirement Theme

Rest assured, thousands of couples dance right into their twilight years without missing a step. Off they go in their RV, out they go on the town, or home they go to just be.

For grins, I'll cite a few of the more difficult adjustments some marriages have had to make because of retirement.

When He Retires

Fishing, golf, woodworking, and travel come to mind. And those things have been on his mind for a long time, especially in the weeks and days leading to his last day on the job. If Honey Pie sits with him in the boat and swats mosquitoes (Boat! a *big* boat!), joins him on the golf course, sits on a stool while he's making a birdhouse (she always knew he could do better than those store-bought ones), or navigates with a map of Arizona in her lap, why, all the better! Life will be blissful and lazy—a one and a two and a one and a two...

He: We'll have coffee together and we'll talk a lot (she always complains I don't talk enough). She'll make an awesome lunch every day, and we'll watch the nightly weather forecast together...not to mention game shows!

How great it will be not to have to shave, to be able to let it all hang out in sweats for a change, to nap when I want. Not that I'll always be resting—no siree—I might just join the guys at the bakeshop, fetch the mail and the paper (yawn), maybe cut the grass (scratch), maybe watch a game or two. The game! Gotta go!

She: There must be a sensitive but clear way to impart this message to him: Stop interrupting me! I've had a lovely dance of my own all these years, and my daily routine is purposeful and defined. All of a sudden, this joker is cutting in.

Excuse me, Honey Bunch, but can't you see I'm busy working? I'm tickled, really—tickled—that you want to engage in conversation, but can it be about something more important than the new truck you saw on the dealer's lot, like world peace or something? And can it be when I'm not engaged in my own work?

I have carved a life for myself for each day of the week. It's a rhythm, a pace. I'm glad you're here, and I share all of your dreams. Truly. I am interested in what you do in your shop and with what you have to say. I want to keep you company—but can I bring a book?

I am not a prop. I am a vital part of your life, of your dreams, but I am also a woman who has many interests and responsibilities, and who needs time to adjust to your constant (and I must be candid) sometimes irritating interruptions. Let me ask you this: How many cans of tomato sauce are in the cupboards? When are the kids' birthdays? The grandkids' birthdays? And when does the dog have to go to the vet? Thought so. I told you...I am a busy person.

I love you, Honey Bunch, but that doesn't mean I'm ready to swat mosquitoes and call it fun.

When She Retires

Clutter control comes to mind. And order. Everything will be cleaned, organized. Books galore to read, gardens galore to tend. And—once and for all—the weight will come off, the facial pores will finally shrink, and there will be time for daily exercise. It will be enlightening, peaceful, and restful. She and hubby will walk along the ocean with white cotton pants rolled up, shoes in hand, with smiles as big as the crescent moon illuminating their path.

He: I don't get it. I mean, didn't she retire so she could devote all of her attention to me, to us? I expected...you know, fresh cookies every day, or *something*. It doesn't feel like much has changed. How come the house still looks the same? She said she was going to clean all the closets, get rid of all this clutter. It's all she talked about: "When I retire *this,* when I retire *that.*" I could not wait to be with her all the time. I don't understand. I mean, we don't even eat dinner at the same time each night anymore.

She: I can't believe I actually held a job and managed to keep the house halfway decent! I mean, I don't know where the time goes, but now that I'm retired, I'm busier than ever. I practically need a palm pilot. It's thrown me off balance, though. When I was working, I rose to the occasion—cooked and cleaned—because I had to. I had a routine that was dictated by the fact that I was gone so long each day. Now, everything is crazy. I wonder if my husband is affected by any of this.

Emotionally Speaking

Emotions galore spring up around retirement time. Let's listen in on a couple who have felt the brunt of these emotions.

She: I could not wait for this moment. All he and I talked about this entire last year was how grand it would be when we were finally together, finally free. As if someone hit a switch, my husband changed. He became ultrasensitive, moody, and disengaged. I was devastated, confused, and angry. We dreamed of this moment, and he was spoiling it. He was like a stranger to me. What happened to us?

He: I thought we'd go into our twilight years hand in hand. But she changed after she retired. She became bossy, intolerant, dissatisfied with everything—apparently even me. I didn't know whether it was some postmenopausal symptom or some big issue surrounding leaving her job of 35 years. I mean, I know she misses her friends and all that, but I'm here. What am I, chopped liver?

> The proper question, perhaps, is not why we have so much divorce, but why we are so unforgiving. The answer, perhaps, is that, though we still recognize the feeling of love, we have forgotten how to practice love when we don't feel it.
>
> **Wendell Berry**

Onward, Christian Spouse

I am a fan of the writings of Wendell Berry, and I encourage you to consider reading one of his many books to hear what this prolific and clear-sighted thinker has to say. The sidebar features a quote from his book *Sex, Economy, Freedom & Community* (Pantheon).

In an essay with the same title, Berry stresses the practice of love through justice, trust, patience, respect, mutual help, and forgiveness. While these virtues are important in any abiding relationship, they are crucial in marriage, especially when someone's marriage is going through a major life transition. These sentiments mirror biblical injunctions on how we are to be toward each other.

I am particularly fond of looking closely at who we are to be as children of light and what happens when we let God the Holy Spirit have His way with us. Specifically, I frequently cite from Ephesians 5 and Galatians 5 in my writings, in hopes to do what little I can to encourage us to walk as children of light.

> For you were once darkness, but now you are light in the Lord. Live as children of light (for fruit of the light consists in all goodness, righteousness and truth) and find out what pleases the Lord. Be careful, then, how you live (Ephesians 5:8-10,15).

> But the fruit of the Spirit is love, joy, peace, patience, kindness, goodness, faithfulness, gentleness and self-control. Against such things there is no law. Those who belong to Christ Jesus have crucified the sinful nature with its passions and desires. Since we live by the Spirit, let us keep in step with the Spirit (Galatians 5:22-25).

Be Careful, Then, How You Live

The manifestation of the fruit of the Spirit must begin at home. If such fruit as love, joy, peace, patience, kindness, goodness, faithfulness, gentleness, and self-control are not manifest between a husband and wife, who call themselves Christians, then they have some serious identity issues.

I simply cannot count how many times I have been shamed by my lack of charity toward my husband—shamed enough to consider myself a big fat phony. And fully human.

Let me put it to you this way: Of all the people in the universe, who do you most want to bless with your earnest efforts to manifest the fruit of the Spirit? You'd better say your husband or your wife!

> We are at our best behavior and our worst behavior at home.
>
> **Rev. Bill Baumgarten**

The apostle Paul just cautioned us in Ephesians to be careful how we live. This book is about living well in retirement. To live well includes living well with others, particularly your mate. In order to live well with the man or woman you married—retired or not—you may have to have a little powwow with yourself, examine your conscience and behavior, and put some effort into living *well*. This is not the time to sit out the dance.

A Big Adjustment

Retirement is a big adjustment, and your marriage will not likely continue as it has always been. Though married (unless you've worked together as a couple all these years), you both have established identities and routines apart from each other.

Suddenly, there he is. Suddenly, there she is. Where once your day had a particular protocol, now it has a particular person. And that person may not jibe with the program.

There is another side to this: Women, in particular, may feel that retirement is finally *their* time to enjoy life, only to find themselves nursing their husband's newfound loss of identity and purpose. For example...

I work at home. Therefore I am always here. Enter Wonder Man. Way cool. I love having Joe around. So here comes the inevitable scenario:

We are both in the same room together, say, reading the paper. I get up to leave, and suddenly it's 20 questions.

"Where are you going?"

Huh?

Why do I have to explain why I'm walking from one room to the next? I feel as if I have to raise my hand to ask permission to go to the bathroom! This can be vexing.

> Haven't you read...that at the beginning the Creator "made them male and female" and said, "For this reason a man will leave his father and mother and be united to his wife, and the two will become one flesh"? So they are no longer two, but one. Therefore what God has joined together, let man not separate.
>
> Matthew 19:4-6

Keep your communication with each other open. That means you both have to talk. Be certain to respect the individual temperament of the other person—and his or her need to go to the bathroom without a grand inquisition.

Married Singles

I've seen them dozens of times and so have you. Maybe you are one yourself—a married single, one-half of a legal contract that has changed your status on paper but has not changed your life in reality. You live your own life and do your own thing, with little regard for your spouse. Oh, you're pleasant enough (though you may have become skillful at using anger to control him or her)—just enough to maintain as comfortable a living arrangement as possible. Some of you really don't care a whit about your mate or about a comfortable relationship. If he or she doesn't like your selfish behavior, the door is always open.

> **vow** \'vaů\ : a solemn promise, pledge, or personal engagement

And now you're facing retirement! *Think* of all the fun things you can do for yourself!

Few of us are as hard-core as that, yet we sometimes slip into this type of behavior, especially because of the demands of work. Work may have kept you away from your core marital relationship. If you've been doing your own thing for a while, you and your mate have mastered a different dance, one that is out of step with your marriage vows.

To be sure, some marriages seem to have originated in some other place than heaven. Some people feel trapped in a loveless and hopeless relationship. Some people are. Invest a moment to examine how you may have contributed to that hopelessness.

A Room of Your Own

For the sake of sound mental health, each person should have his or her own space. Having a place you can call your own is a good thing—a place where you can surround yourself with those things that bring you comfort or joy, a place where you can stash personal, private treasures.

> He doesn't have ulcers—he's a carrier.

Stump Time!

1. Have I fostered resentment from my spouse?

2. Why have I fostered resentment?

3. Do I see the speck of dust in her or his eye and miss the log in mine? (Spend extra time on the stump with this question.)

4. These are my honest-to-goodness personality flaws:

5. If I expect my mate to accept my flaws, why am I so persistently intolerant of his or hers?

6. Never mind what I see wrong in my spouse. How can *I* change?

7. Does stubborn determination to prove myself right override the love I claim to have for my husband or wife?

Many couples have established their own turf throughout the life of their marriage. Typically, the woman finds refuge in the kitchen (Joe, who shares kitchen duties happily, still does not know where everything goes when he empties the dishwasher.) The man often has a shop or a garage.

I am advocating for a specific space: a spare bedroom that can be converted to a craft room or a reading room, a corner of the shop or garage that can be partitioned for an official fly-tying room, or a showcase for one's woodworking hobby. Space. Even a special space outdoors. A place to call your own.

> In relationships, just as in every other aspect of life, the spirit and attitude with which you do things are at least as important as your actual actions.
>
> **Dr. Phil McGraw**

Attitude!

Look at Dr. McGraw's quote. There's that attitude issue again!

I just wrote about walking as children of light and quoted from Galatians.

The apostle Paul was telling the Galatians what the profile of a Christian is—attitude supreme. Let's look at the preceding verses, where he outlines the profile of a child of darkness:

> The acts of the sinful nature are obvious: sexual immorality, impurity and debauchery; idolatry and witchcraft; hatred, discord, jealousy, fits of rage, selfish ambition, dissensions, factions and envy; drunkenness, orgies, and the like. I warn you, as I did before, that those who live like this will not inherit the kingdom of God (Galatians 5:19-21).

What scuttles your ship? Throw it overboard. Put things like anger and resentment and selfishness and hatred and impurity in a chest and pitch it. Swab the deck clean. Replace that which is negative and sinful in your life with positive virtue. How? *Let the Holy Spirit have His way with you.* It's totally possible…you *can* teach an old dog new tricks. We're supposed to be new creatures in Christ, remember?

Compromise

An apt definition for *relationship* could be "compromise."

- I am in an amazing *compromise* with the man of my dreams.
- My wife and I have a terrific *compromise.*

There is no way around it. Every single one of us has individual quirks, personalities, life experiences, cultural imperatives, and let's just say "background noise." Regardless how alike some people can be, every one is different.

Difference is good! Life would be flatline *boring* if we all were the same. One person's hollow spots can make a good fit with the other's lumps. You have nothing to fit to if you're the same. Think of a magnet. Also think of the old adage "Opposites attract."

If you were both the same, you might as well dance alone. A mirror would be all the equipment you'd need for a partner. Everything you said would be rubber-stamped with smiley faces and stars. *Please!*

Difference is hard! It's not only hard, difference can drive us batty. For your information, that is why the word *compromise* was invented in the first place—so we wouldn't all end up throwing mashed potatoes and peas at each other at the funny farm. Compromise was cooked up to preserve our sanity.

Joe and I are exact opposites. If I were ever on a game show and a million dollars was at stake to guess how my husband would react to a certain stimulus, I'd bring home the gold. I would merely answer with the exact opposite of how I would react. A perfect example of our differences occurred this morning.

The day promised to be torrid by Montana standards: mid 90s and tinder dry—the kind of weather that causes us all to look toward our heavily forested mountains with anxiety.

Keeping with the advice I've given *in at least three books*, I closed windows and shades on the east, south, and west exposures of our home early in the morning, keeping north windows and curtains open. I have practiced this method for keeping the house cool for years.

All of a sudden I walk into our north-facing living room, and it's a tomb: windows closed and heavy drapes drawn. Joe was humming and going about his business.

Claustrophobia hit me like a tsunami.

"What are you doing?" I croaked.

"Shutting up the house," he said merrily, "to keep it cool."

"That's not the way I do it," I responded, with enough ice on my words to cool the house for a week.

"Oh—you don't do it right," he said breezily, not yet aware of the hole he was digging.

"Joseph! I write *books* about this stuff!"

By now he figured out his dilemma, whipped back the drapes, thrust open the windows, and stomped downstairs.

Hours later, we can laugh at this as well as engage in a little analysis:

1. I was performing my predetermined ritual.

2. My ego was wrapped tightly in my ritual.

3. Joseph was merely taking initiative and doing what was perfectly natural now that he was home to do it.

4. There wasn't a reason in heaven or on earth why he should have checked with me before he performed his ritual.

5. Difference in opinion can surface at a time like this.

6. That's all it is: difference in opinion.

7. The moral of this is that if you don't compromise, you'll go nuts. Or claustrophobic.

Hop in the Hay

You heard me right: restore your sexual activity. I've read that sexual intimacy between husband and wife becomes more fulfilling as we grow older. There are obvious reasons for this:

1. We tend to be more relaxed with our bodies and with who we are.

2. We are empty-nested.

3. We have time and no longer face exhaustion from tiring routines.

The benefits of an active sex life are quite astounding, actually. Doctors at the Royal Edinburgh Hospital interviewed thousands of patients to discover that older people with a regular sex life looked younger, felt better, had less stress, and slept better.

Declining sexual function can be cause for both frustration and humiliation. Without question, our bodies change as hormones ebb and flow. A visit with your doc should remedy any physical problems or discomfort. (It is worth noting that sexual performance can be affected negatively by certain drugs, both prescription and over-the-counter.)

> When we're happy with our lives, we're more fulfilled sexually.
>
> **Karen Donohy, Ph.D.**

The Christian marriage has long been a symbol of the mystery of Christ and His church, and when a loving marriage is sealed through intimacy, the husband and wife are part of this mystery. Marriage becomes a living allegory of Christ's love for the church and the church's love for Christ. This is such an important message that I implore you to read this paragraph again.

Sexual relations are the core of the marital union, and expressions of sex outside of this union are forbidden. This is not because of some sort of strict, uptight Puritanical ethic, but because adultery violates the integrity of the allegory that marriage is.

I was struck dumb when a recent president was accused of adultery. Talking heads and pundits rallied, pro and con.

Pro: "You don't really think he's the first! After all, men will be men!"

Con: "It was a dereliction of duty, right there in the White House!"

For my two cents' worth, nobody got it right.

Here's the way I look at it: How could I feel trust for a civic leader who cannot maintain fidelity toward *the one person he loves above all others?* Toward the person to whom he committed himself in a solemn vow? I am distressed mightily by how we have trivialized the deep significance of intimacy between a husband and a wife.

Scripture supports this exclusive sexual relationship in such verses as Hebrews 13:4; 1 Corinthians 6:12-20; and 1 Thessalonians 4:3-7. Scripture also tells husband and wife to delight in each other. Hey, Wonder Man!

It may be an error in judgment to expect a repeat honeymoon two seconds after you wake up and smell the coffee—and now have the time to drink it together. Patience! Ease into each other's embrace again, and get rid of that roommate status.

For Your Funny Bone

Just to loosen you up a bit for the next topic, I'm reproducing a few fifth-grade students' answers to test questions that I found on the Internet, which have absolutely nothing to do with retirement but are a good segue to a discussion on humor.

- Solomon had 300 wives and 700 porcupines. He was a hysterical figure as well as being in the Bible. It sounds like he was sort of busy too.

- Sir Francis Drake circumcised the world with a 100-foot clipper which was very dangerous to all his men.

- Joan of Arc was burned to a steak and was canonized by Bernard Shaw for reasons I don't really understand. The English and French still have problems.

And how about what has been cited as the world's funniest joke:

> Sherlock Holmes and Dr. Watson are camping. They pitch their tent under the stars and go to sleep. Sometime in the middle of the night, Holmes wakes Watson up: "Watson, look up at the stars and tell me what you deduce."
>
> Watson says, "I see millions of stars, and even if a few of those have planets, it's quite likely there are some planets like Earth. And if there are a few planets like Earth out there, there might also be life."
>
> Holmes replies, "Watson, you idiot, somebody stole our tent."

If you're not laughing out loud after that, I recommend you see a doctor—you may be dead.

Find Your Funny Bone

I write a humor column, and with certain people (namely my two sisters), I can be downright funny. Lots of people think of me as funny because of my public persona. There are times when I laugh myself silly. I can also be downright dour. Dour rhymes with sour. A key aspect of humor is to *not* take oneself so seriously.

While I need more practice at what I preach, I believe a sense of humor is important for our mental and physical health. (One of my resolutions every year is to laugh more.)

By humor I do not mean teasing, which can be merciless and mean-spirited. By humor I mean two things: (1) to laugh out loud because you are happy, and (2) to stop being poised to be offended or hurt at every turn and to loosen up a lot. (If we spent any appreciable time on our stump we'd probably figure out that we ourselves are very funny creatures.)

> God cannot endure that unfestive, mirthless attitude of ours in which we eat our bread in sorrow, with pretentious, busy haste, or even with shame. Through our daily meals He is calling us to rejoice, to keep holiday in the midst of our working day.
>
> **Dietrich Bonhoeffer**
>
> May I paraphrase the last part?
>
> He is calling us to rejoice, to keep holiday in our retirement.

My Joe has an unsophisticated sense of humor. Primitive, childlike jokes crack him up. (Cantaloupe? Then lettuce marry. My heart beets for you. Orange you glad we met?) This is my undoing. Rather than laugh with him, I glare. *How can you possibly find that funny at your age* is written all over my face, as is my state-of-the-art disapproving stare when anything goes awry.

Note to me: Chill out!

Note to Joe: Go ahead and laugh yourself silly.

Note to you: Find your funny bone.

You don't stop laughing because you grow old. You grow old because you stop laughing.

Dancing the Night Away

Relationships have a rosy side in retirement. Let me share what Wonder Man and I have learned:

- an awesome early morning comfort when you first awaken and don't have to jump out of bed, but can linger in each other's arms

- the lovely little courtesies you can spoil each other with: scratching a back, fetching a refill on the lemonade, sharing a task, relieving the other of a chore

- the spontaneous moments when you can sit in a favorite spot and talk

- the time for more physical intimacy (something Joe and I overlooked due to exhaustion, time constraints, and medical issues...dumb us)

- trips to town with lists and the shared adventure of shopping
- reading out loud to each other
- more time to pray together
- working at adjoining desks and listening to (gulp) country music (This is definitely a case where I've compromised!)
- eating lunch al fresco and spitting olive pits over the deck rail
- walking down the lane together to fetch the paper
- talking to grandchildren on the phone—the both of us—and singing songs from *The Sound of Music* long-distance
- dreaming about tomorrow while being fully and peacefully alive today

How to Make Your Marriage Rumba

I've devised some not-so-retiring ideas to strengthen your marriage. Each of these projects comes with instructions and bonus points. Though written to enhance your marriage as you enter retirement, these suggestions could apply to marriages of any age.

Rule Number One: Learn to Listen.
Rule Number Two: Listen.

We are all guilty. Whether it is a private little distraction, the rigmarole of daily drudge and routine, our preoccupation with a project, a TV show, or a good book, we become so focused with our own moment that we neglect our partner's plea: Listen to me! We may think we are listening, but do we hear? One sure way to restore intimacy to your marriage is to listen to your mate and hear the message of the words.

The reflex is as mechanical as breathing: Our partner talks and we nod. We say "uh-huh" and "oh" and "really," rote words that come from practice that comes from accustomed comfort. It is a lazy comfort that requires little investment from us as our eyes remain riveted on the TV, on the paper, or off in space while we think of other matters. Yet those unengaged eyes of ours betray us. Our spouse knows it and we know it as words bounce off us and land in the ever-widening gap between us. Yet we both settle for this customary response, always wishing to be heard.

Ask yourself, *Do I pay attention when my spouse talks to me?*

Pledge to hear with your heart. Interesting, isn't it, that *hear*ing is buried inside our *heart*?

Here is a project: Initiate dialogue with your mate. Show interest. Turn off the TV. Look into each other's eyes when talking. Ask pertinent questions to show that you are hearing what is said.

Here is some practice: Set aside time this evening for a heart-to-heart talk about your marriage. Don't discuss the difficult parts. Use the time to say why you are so glad to be married to each other.

Here is the bonus:

1. The greatest compliment you can pay another person is to show respect for his or her opinions.

2. You will both come to view yourselves as each other's best friends. (Best friends listen!)

3. You will each feel your comments have worth.

Love Letters

Some of us never say it, and some of us say it a lot: "I love you." It is a good thing to hear, and it is an especially good thing to be certain about. Love within a marriage is deep and abiding. Lack of love, though, can be hurtful as individual temperaments rub the surface of marital love raw. Words of love bring a soothing assurance. Without love, differences stick out like stinging nettles.

Love within a marriage can be challenging. Expressions of marital love are often swept aside by hectic lifestyles (even when retired!), exhaustion, and personality clashes. When a marriage faces a triumph or tragedy, love binds it together. But when triumph and tragedy wane, we often resort to predictable expressions of affection—or none at all.

Ask yourself this: *We love each other, but have we ever taken the time to explain why?*

Pledge to guard against neglecting your love for each other.

Here's a project: Write a love letter right now. The letter could begin with the sentence "I love you because you are_____."
The letter could end with the sentence "I'm so glad you are my_____, because you make me feel_____."

Here's some practice: Vary your love letters by writing a poem or a story about your mate.

Here's a bonus:

1. You may be less inclined to take each other for granted.
2. You will each be uplifted by private words of affection.
3. Self-esteem will soar.

Thanks for the Compliments

"Familiarity breeds contempt," the old wag goes. Witness the behavior of some people joined in holy wedlock, and the adage seems true! One particularly uncivil practice that seems to come from familiarity is the tendency to publicly ridicule or to tease.

Teasing can be fun. It can also be carried too far. When it is carried too far it is unmerciful, sometimes caustic, and always hurtful. "You always hurt the one you love," croons the golden oldie. (Don't dance to that song!) How true, how tragic, and how strange that those who pledge love and fidelity to each other would choose instead to be cruel.

Perhaps teasing is not so much a choice but a pattern developed for want of something else to say. If so, take time to develop kinder habits, those that edify and build your partner's esteem. Few methods accomplish this chore as successfully as *genuine* public edification of each other.

What man would not feel proud when his wife sincerely applauded his efforts in front of others? What woman would not feel goose bumps when her husband praised her talents in front of others?

Ask yourself this: *When was the last time my remarks about my spouse were edifying?*

Pledge to keep your lips sealed in public if you cannot say something nice about your mate.

Here's a project: Listen to the conversation of others. Watch the body language of couples who openly speak of their affection and appreciation for each other. Then watch the reaction of those who resort to insensitive teasing.

Here's some practice: Make it a point to say something grand about your spouse the next time you are in the company of others.

Here's a bonus:

1. You will feel appreciated by each other.

2. You will be more careful of what you say in public.

3. Others may take your cue.

Give a Massage

Massage can be healing, restorative, invigorating—and seductive. There is no question that touch belongs in the repertoire of lovers!

The Bible sanctifies touch between husband and wife. Turn to the Song of Solomon and read: "My lover is mine and I am his." Or listen to the apostle Paul as he celebrates the intimacy of marriage when he reminds men and women that their bodies belong to each other. We were made for intimate touch.

To be sure, massage is a practical boon to health, but it is also a critical component to lovemaking. (Although some massage puts people more in the mood for *sleep* than sexual encounter. Or it hurts. When Joe massages my lower back, my screams can be heard as far away as Detroit!)

There are physical and psychological benefits to massage. Feeling the loving and sure touch of your lover brings emotional support and bonds you in confident trust. After all, we are most vulnerable when lying under the strokes and reassuring touch of another. Inhibition, sensitivity, and anxiety over touch all interfere with a full and satisfying expression of marital love.

Ask yourself this: *If I am too inhibited to let my spouse massage my body, how about starting with a "safe" area, such as my head?*

Pledge to explore your partner's entire body with gentle (and warm) hands.

Here's a project: Invest in an erotically-scented massage oil. Dim the bedroom lights or use some candles. Play soothing music. Massage your mate beginning with the feet and working to the top of the head. (Well…see if you can make it all the way to the top of the head….) Let your willingness to be close come through your hands as you pass nonverbal communication to the one you love.

Here's some practice: Learn to give a spot massage by rubbing hands, feet, or temples.

Here's a bonus:

1. You will begin to fully appreciate the deep, sexual love that is found in the Song of Solomon.

2. Both of you will experience release from stress.

3. You will deepen trust.

Some Additional Ways to Put Intimacy into Your Marriage

- Don't just say "I love you" and drop the subject. Tonight say "I love you because…."

- Contrive a gesture, a word, a certain glance that is a secret code of love in public.

- Attach a love note to his steering wheel, to the mane of her favorite horse, to the bathroom mirror.

- Get a small, sturdy paper bag with a handle. Write "Isle of View" (I Love You) on the side. The holder of the bag is responsible for the next "surprise" gift. It's in the bag.

- Let the answering machine handle the phone.

- Militantly guard yourselves from too much extracurricular activity. Run into each other's arms instead of to meetings and social obligations.

- Smile with your eyes.

- Turn on the "June Bugs"—a little tickle in the right place is good to reduce stress. Just don't be annoying about this.

- Watch a funny video together.

- Don't get aggravated—get humor.

- Set an appointment for love, and build to the moment with special, private language.

- Clean sheets.

- Clean bodies. No face stubble, no hairy legs.

- Candles—in a safe spot, in something to collect the meltdown. Use only real wax candles or soy candles. The synthetic ones are not healthy for you.

- Music. The kind that is meaningful to both of you. Praise and worship music is an excellent choice.

- Aroma. Get an essential oil lamp and burn ylang-ylang or lavender.

- Get into that slinky number. He won't mind if you fill it out a bit more.

- Perfumed bodies—the both of you.

- Take your time.

- Don't stop listening now!

- Afterward, keep connected with touch.

- Give thanks to God for the gift of intimacy.

- Tell each other how terrific you feel.

- Sweet dreams!

A Love Story

Years ago I wrote a newspaper column about dear friends of ours. I am offering the story of Jim and Gracie as incentive for us all to grab our partner's hand and to live well—together—in retirement.

ℋolding ℋands

He was oak; she was willow. Big-boned and thick, he towered over her delicate, elfin body. Yet oh, how Jim loved Gracie, and how Gracie rose to the occasion! They were salt and pepper, horse and carriage, complete only as a set, perfect in their awkward dissimilarity—Jim was steel beam, Gracie cotton field. Yet they were inseparable. Where one was, you'd find the other—Jim and Grace, Grace and Jim, always together, linked by the simple act of holding hands.

Jim had a way of cupping Gracie's hand in that huge paw of his. His fingers too thick to lace with hers, he took her hand reverently and placed it carefully against his palm, closing his fist around his treasure, a bird too delicate to fly alone. That is how Jim held Gracie's hand, and that is how they always were. Visions of them cruising the mall, heading into a café for early dinner, walking back from their rural mailbox, sitting on their couch—the giant and the bird, linked together by such a simple act.

Age began to creep alongside that ungainly couple, crumpling Gracie's spine, putting pause in her walk, punching her breath into disjointed gasp, yet she kept her post beside Jim's hulking, stooped, and failing body; pain the giant in their lives now, closing *its* brutal fist around the inseparable couple.

With limp, with pause, with shuffle where once there were determined steps, they held on for dear life, elfin hand gulfed in massive mitt. She looked to him for strength, for assurance. *You are safe with me, Gracie, I will never let you go.* And yet he did let go. Jim answered the call that finally comes to all, his huge body at its final rest, to lumber alongside his Gracie no more.

Gracie sits alone on her couch now, Jim's spot empty, her hand curled in a limpid fist on floral print pattern. Her emptiness is as huge as his presence once was, their perfect set broken, the sorrow unbearable for a little bird who was always too delicate to fly alone.

May we all share a love like Gracie's and Jim's.

6

Of a Mind (and Heart) to Retire

CYNTHIA:

"He's not too heavy in the saddle," Joe will say about a man he feels does not pull his weight.

"About as sharp as the edge of town," is his comment about someone's mental acuity.

What about him? What about Joe Yates' mental acuity? Joe is one of the smartest people I've ever encountered. He has a native intelligence that cuts to the core of any issue with a wisdom and certainty that can be unnerving. His mind is like a computer with endless data. This can be good and bad.

Joe has benefited from his raw intelligence and common sense, and he has become an absolute wizard when tackling the mundane or the legal jargon of dry contractual language. And in matters of brain function or emotional stability, Joe thrives on routine.

Backing into the same parking space at work every morning for 37 years brought him huge comfort. To suddenly bear the responsibility of creating a *new* comfortable routine seems daunting for Joe. To keep himself busy and active is easy; to channel his thoughts into meaningful patterns during a patternless time is not. I sense that my husband's "data" is as compartmentalized as was his life for all those years. To suddenly be cut free from daily rote may be unsettling for him.

JOE:

When I planned for retirement, I set certain goals. Once I reached those goals, I could retire. But as the magic day approached, I began to look at the big picture: What could I trade off and still walk out the door when I want to? Most employers do not set an age for mandatory retirement. So any mandate is of our own doing, as are most of our goals.

I always knew that at a certain age and after a certain number of years of service, I could retire and probably would. The question for me was, what would I be and what would I do? I don't think that I expected to go straight from one job to another, even part-time, but I did want to be able to do something else. One of my expressions is "You're burning daylight," so if the sun is up I feel I should be doing something. The greater question for me has become, does God have a plan for my day?

Free

"Your mind is now free to follow your feet." I like that.

I don't know where I read these words, but they have stuck with me. I'm not at all certain the original context had anything to do with retirement, but the words are fitting. Your mind is now free of the multitude of thoughts, responsibilities, and pressures that defined your life for so long.

Remember Etch A Sketch? That red plastic box kept us occupied for hours as we turned knobs to make houses and ponies and flowers and stick men. (Ever try to write your name in cursive on one of those things?) How did we erase our artistic masterpieces? We shook the dickens out of that box until all the black soot fell into some sort of Etch A Sketch holding tank, whereupon we would start again.

That is a good analogy for what's happened to the thoughts that have dominated your mind for so long.

- You no longer have to agonize over how you will get through the annual rating of a particularly difficult employee. (When his IQ reaches 50, he should sell.)

- You no longer have to wonder if you finished your quarterly report with accuracy.

- You don't even have to think about what you will wear, what you will eat for lunch, or when you will take vacation.

It's all shook up.

This chapter is dedicated to your mind and emotions—to keeping your thinking on the right track and to keeping your brain healthy. The "healthy" part of this equation rests heavily on all of us boomers as we face our uncertain futures with many possibilities in front of us. Mental clarity is not the least of our concerns. (And that concern is valid.)

Don't Retire Your Mind

Just because you've left the brain drain of your job and you won't be using your mind for usual modus operandi, you won't stop using it altogether. For one thing, you will be using your mind a lot while considering whether to retire.

I'm going to look at four aspects of this issue: the decision process, the reprogramming process, the reconnecting process, and the maintenance process.

The Decision Process

We make decisions every day. Some of our decisions stand alone and have significant impact on our lives: education, marriage, relocation, children, career, retirement. We make decisions that lead to addiction or to sin. We make decisions that favorably alter our lives. Every informed person on this planet must make a decision whether to accept or reject Jesus Christ. We not only decide to act in a certain way, or to do some thing, we decide how we are going to respond to changes or consequences as a result of our decisions. As a society that values independence, decision making becomes an enormous burden as we each face a maddening array of possible options. This can be a very lonely place to be.

Two aspects of our decision making are worth mentioning here. One is the way in which we mull around an idea and evaluate its merit, and the other is our worry over whether we made the right decision.

Evaluating and Bringing Clarity to Your Thoughts

Does the phrase "weighing heavily on your mind" generate any response from you? It should. Deciding to retire is a mighty big step.

You have used your mind to calculate and to crunch figures. And you have used it to think long and hard about whether or not to retire. Making the decision, signing the papers, giving notice, and making your intentions public are all results of thinking. Maintaining clarity through this thinking process is critically important. One way to keep your mind focused on the big question is to ask yourself other questions:

- Do I feel…never mind feel—do I *know* deep down inside that it is time to go?

- Have I considered the social, financial, and mental fallout from retirement?

- Have I discussed this with my spouse, and is she or he on the same page?

- Do I have my ducks lined up? Are finances pretty stable?

- Do I have a network of friends or a support system on hand if I need propping during this process?

- What can I do to make this process positive and to keep worry to a minimum?

Worry

The bottom line about retirement is that you have to decide whether it will be a crisis, a challenge, or a cakewalk. You can control the way you perceive this transition. If worry seems unavoidable, listen to this: Worry leads to stress, and we all know what stress leads to—a really taxing, toxic mix for your overall health, both mental and physical. You may agree in principle with the caution to stay clear of worry and yet worry all the same. Welcome to the world of being fully human.

Jesus told us plain and clear, however, that worry doesn't get us a bit closer to solutions of the issue at hand. He told us not to worry. In Matthew 6:27-34, He said this:

> After all, you don't worry about good things, you worry about the bad.
>
> **Ryan M. Wigness**

> Who of you by worrying can add a single hour to his life? And why do you worry about clothes? See how the lilies of the field grow. They do not labor or spin. Yet I tell you that not even Solomon in all his splendor was dressed like one of these. If that is how God clothes the grass of the field, which is here today and tomorrow is thrown into the fire, will he not much more clothe you, O you of little faith? So do not worry, saying "What shall we eat?" or "What shall we drink?" or "What shall we wear?" For the pagans run after all these things, and your heavenly Father knows that you need them. But seek first his kingdom and his righteousness, and all these things will be given to you as well. Therefore do not worry about tomorrow, for tomorrow will worry about itself. Each day has enough trouble of its own.

Oswald Chambers, known for his devotional *My Utmost for His Highest,* is a tad less charitable: "Fretting," he wrote, "springs from a determination to get our own way."

Now there's something to ponder on our stump!

Yet worry we all do. I haven't yet met a soul who has not fretted over something, whether it's the day's forecast (got to get on those links, you know), the health of another person, his or her own health, finances, or a relationship turned sour. We try to heed Jesus' counsel, but worry seems to be built into our very corpuscles. I'd venture to say if we ran across someone who croons, "Don't worry, be happy" all the time we'd consider that person a candidate for either Fake o' the Year or the loony bin.

I admit to worry. I worry about my health, my husband (when Wonder Man gets on the seat of his Massey-Ferguson tractor, I'm in a dither until he returns in one piece), our son and his wife. I worry about our grandchildren, my mother and sisters, our pets, the farm animals…not to mention world peace, the safety of our food supply, those who are marginalized in society, people who are suffering for want of food or liberty, terrorism, the AIDS epidemic….

I believe the difference between my worry and worry that might cripple me is that, for the most part, it does not consume me (except when Tractor Man is rumbling over hill and dale). It may be that my worry would be better categorized as concern.

wor·ry \'wǝr-ē\ : to feel uneasy or anxious; to fret; to torment oneself with or suffer from disturbing thoughts

ε٠

con·cern \kǝn-'sǝrn\ : matter that engages one's attention, interest, or care

What would Jesus say about *concern*? He certainly seemed to be concerned about a lot of things—our salvation, to name a biggie.

I'm thinking Jesus would be okay with concern. I hope so because I think you *should* be concerned about retiring. It's a big step. Retirement must grab your concentrated attention, and you should care about your future emotional, physical, spiritual, and financial security. I've gone to great lengths to actually promote healthy concern throughout this book. It might even be irresponsible not to care about such matters. Just don't push concern past the edge of that lily field.

Let's look at those three possible responses when facing retirement: crisis, challenge, or cakewalk.

A Crisis

Some people are career worriers and have turned worry into an art form. That worry can paralyze them with fear. Proverbs 12:25 reminds us that an anxious heart weighs a man down. The burden of fear is far too heavy for us to carry, especially at a time in our life when our mind is supposedly "free to follow our feet."

The best way I know to confront your worries and fears is to meet them head-on. By confrontation, I mean praying to seek the help and mercy of God, thinking hard, and digging deeply to find the root cause of our fears.

Stump Time!

Spend time with each of the following comments. Peel away as many layers as you can and try to get to the bottom of your fear.

- Of course retirement is a big step. That is no surprise. But gazillions of other people have gone through the process. What is it about retiring that has me scared witless?

- Why am I driving myself nuts trying to finalize my decision? What loss am I afraid to face? Is it identity? Power? Money? Purpose?

- Does the thought of an uncertain, uncharted future scare the tar out of me? Am I even able to "let my mind follow my feet"?

- Am I willing to accept that I have really limited vision right now, that God's grace and leading will bring me to new vistas and show me things about this world, about life, about my mate, and about myself that I'd never dreamed?

- Can I talk with a trusted friend or a pastor about this seemingly unnatural fear that is devouring me? Who would that be?

Depression

Keeping in mind that a qualified mental health professional might say I have rocks in my head, I believe that some depression is healthy.

Frankly, I believe some depression is part of a healing response to certain experiences. For instance, I am depressed when Wonder Man and I aren't getting along well. I would *definitely* be depressed if something happened to him, or to anyone else I love. (Like, I'm supposed to not worry, to just be happy, if something happens to a loved one? Not this chick. And probably not you.)

> Wearing a uniform or a badge does not make you immune to normal human emotion.
>
> U.S. Surgeon General
> Dr. Richard Carmona

You may be depressed for a while after you retire. Big deal. The morning is coming when you will wake up, fix your hair again or shave, and "follow your feet" into that great big life ahead of you. In the meantime, go sit on the couch and eat bonbons. It's only for a while; you might as well enjoy yourself.

(A handful of men, including my husband, who worked alongside each other for decades all "cluster" retired within a year. They meet each month for lunch. This is a healthy and necessary association that can stem the tide of depression. Close relationships ground us.)

Some of you reading this have catapulted into a black hole. You may be suffering from melancholy or despair from any number of causes, and you may be utterly miserable. Worry and fear have grabbed you by the throat and flung you onto the ground in full-out depression. You need some good news. Here it is: You are reading this book right now. Talk about a faithful God! Your depression matters to Him.

God knows your heart, my friend. He knows your past. He knows your future. He knows what makes you tick. He knows every single hair on your head—and what makes those hairs stand on end. Because He knows you so well, He put this book, this very page and these very words, in your hands. That reality can help you smile and lift some of your depression.

But some of us cannot "fix" depression with a cute phrase, with determination to overcome, or with a writer's cheering and goodwill. Some people have brains wired from birth that don't transmit positive feelings too well. Some people have hormonal imbalances. Some people have food allergies or other allergies. Some people get out of balance emotionally as a result of an outside stimulus, often some sort of personal shake-up or tragedy.

> Depression has been called the number one reversible cause of memory loss in the elderly.

An article in *Parade* magazine by Diana Holes and Robert E. Holes states that depressed men are two to four times more likely to take their own lives than depressed women. The relentless agony of depression, the authors say, may make suicide seem like the only way out. In that article, Dr. John Greden, director of the University of Michigan Depression Center, states, "All the while the depression goes untreated, it is causing ongoing damage that may shrivel important regions of the brain."

If depression lasts longer than a short while, please go talk to a professional. It does not make sense to put yourself and those around you through this. Black holes are no fun. I know—I've been in a few myself.

Strong Warning

Depression can lead to suicide. Statistics inform us that suicide is a growing issue during retirement years, especially with older men. If you or someone you know has suicidal thoughts or makes mention of suicide, seek professional help at once. Period. No middle ground. Promise me.

A Challenge

Retirement? Hah! I can tackle this baby! Step aside, 'cause all I've got to do is decide to do it, and that's that! Willpower is my forte. I can do anything when I set my mind to it.

Is this the way you handle life? Way to go, Lone Ranger! But it might be the wrong way to go. Let me explain:

Challenges are good for us—probably healthy for us. Many of us like to be "up to the challenge." But consider two things:

1. Where is "submitting your will to God and turning to Him for help" in all of this bravado?
2. What happens when you meet the challenge? A lot of people are so challenge driven that they don't know what to do when they accomplish the task.

> **P**ride is a kind of pleasure produced by a man thinking too well of himself.
>
> **Baruch Spinoza**

Retirement is a challenge, no bones about it. If you have roll-up-your-sleeves gumption, all the better. Just remember that pride goeth before a fall. If you take this life transition as a challenge, don't do it in a vacuum, but do so in concert with God and with others, which, in a sense, you are already doing if you're reading this book.

A Cakewalk

You lucky ones! You manage to slide through life's transitions as if you were coated with Teflon. More than likely you have a positive, half-full-glass attitude, a sunny disposition, and a yearning to go Godward. Good for you! And happy trails.

Reprogram

If your thoughts are cut in stone, inflexible, and made up for life, watch out: Your times, they are a changin'. You will soon experience the reprogramming of your mind-set, your internal clock, and your ego. You have to—you're not at work anymore.

It's All in Your Head

Much of what you have read in this book has pointed to one rather basic fact: You are going to have to make a mental adjustment in order to live well during your retirement years. The fact that you are reading this book (and others, I hope) means that you are well on your way to this necessary transformation. There is no escaping the fact that you are going to have to reprogram that noggin of yours regardless of your identity, your attitude, and your plans. Here are three exercises that might help with your mental adjustment.

Write

A notebook or a journal might be a smart purchase for you right now, not so much to get all starry-eyed and write your memoirs (though that is a great idea…more on that later) but to give coherence to your mental maneuvering. Outlining ideas on paper seems to animate them and give them a greater importance and voice. When written, your thoughts jump into their first phase of life, that "hatching" concept we've heard about, as in "hatching a plan."

Read

Feed your mind with as much data as you can find that will have an impact on your specific plans, goals, or dreams—information that will likely help you understand what you might

Even in his last years, Grandpappy had a mind like a steel trap, but it had been out so long it had rusted shut.

want to reach for or to dream about. This does not mean a mile-high pile of books identical to this. Look to other books or magazines that cover areas in which you've expressed interest.

- For instance, if you truly want to travel, start with a few travel magazines, write to chambers of commerce, and haunt the travel section of your local bookstore. (Joe and I have developed a hobby through the years: we buy the *Off the Beaten Path* book for each state in which we will spend time. Our goal is to cross off every place mentioned in bold. We are about a third of the way through Montana, our home state.)

- Suppose you have always wanted to tool leather. See if you can find one of the many correspondence courses available and begin to learn about tanning hides and working with leather.

- Suppose about all the culinary skill you have is to heat a frozen pizza or to microwave popcorn. (Not so good for your health, Honey Bunch.) Dust off one of those several thousand cookbooks languishing on your shelves and join your wife in the kitchen. Matter of fact, send her out of the kitchen. (More on "what to do" in chapter 9.)

Think

Put in some serious stump time. Or sit on a dock. Or on a street bench. Or in a church. Or in a garden. You get the idea. Sit a spell and think a while. Just think. Clear your mind of all the racket that's been clamoring for so long and just sit. Make yourself think about this significant change that is taking place. Have a sort of "Retiremental Meditation" session with yourself. Different from your resolute exercise to write your thoughts and plans, this is a time to slow way, way down, with no specific thoughts in sight.

Reset Your Clocks

I heard of a man who never had an alarm clock. This man traveled far and wide but always arrived at airports or meetings on time—all with his internal clock.

I look at it this way: We have an instinctive, regulatory, automatic internal clock (which is defined by science as our circadian rhythm) and a trained, habituated, internal clock. But you don't have to be at work at 9:00 A.M. any longer. Routine has abruptly stopped. Understand this in your head first.

Understand that getting "all dressed up with no place to go" may result in a bit of panic, discomfiture, or confusion. The daily drudge is over. Kaput. Past tense. Time to establish a new rhythm, to set your clock anew. Don't try to do this overnight. Ease into this, and as you begin to reset your internal clocks you will learn to prioritize your days wisely.

You should also wrap your head around another time-related issue. To make my point, I am going to share a short story from two years ago…to this day.

I am drafting this part of the book on July 12, 2004—my fifty-seventh birthday. It is 11:00 A.M. Montana time. *Exactly* two years ago to this day and this very minute (10:00 A.M California time), Joe and I were sitting in the office of the Episcopal Bishop of Northern California, in Sacramento. I was there specifically to discuss the possibility (or merits) of a more specific form of ministry. I remember looking Bishop Lamb in the eyes and saying, "Today is my fifty-fifth birthday. As long as my health remains good, I have a minimum of 20 years of active service ahead." How many years do you have at a minimum?

Our culture once looked at 55 as a threshold to "old." Now it is nothing more than a casual nod at midlife with a slight shuffle toward what many are calling our third age.

I am not convinced that we will, should, or *could* mimic our parents' retirement any longer. Standards have changed in the way we live, in the way we feel, and in the endless possibilities that loom before us. Try this little exercise on for size:

> I have (at a minimum) _____ years ahead of me. I recognize the spiritual imperative to be a wise steward of everything (including time). While I hope to enjoy my retirement and do the following _____, I think I could best steward those years by also_____ _____.

Let me know how it went.

In his book *Here and Now* (Crossroad General Interest), the late Henri Nouwen wrote, "When I was thirty, I said: 'I can easily live another thirty!' When I was forty, I mused, 'Maybe I am only halfway!' Today I can no longer say that, and my question has become: 'How am I going to use the few years left to me?'"

Drive, Motivation, and Control

Time to shift gears on that driveshaft because you just made a major turn. If you are facing a hill, you need to downshift to get up or to get down. I suspect you won't be on cruise control for a while—too many of those road signs on your route right now.

The way we think affects our drive and motivation. For example, you may be too comfortable to get out of bed in the morning, but you reason, *If I lie here another half hour, then I will have to skip such and such. Or I can add an extra half hour at the end of the day for chores.*

Flip it inside out, and you are still driven by your thoughts: *If I lie here another half hour, I'll never accomplish those things I meant to accomplish today, and I'll be on a dead run all morning. Drats, better get out of bed.*

Self motivating is downright hard—take it from one who writes for a living! If you have trouble motivating yourself, tape this Latin phrase to your mirror: *Incipe: Dimidium facti est coepisse.* It translates like this: "Begin. Half the work is in the starting." (I'd say the other half is in the finishing!)

You have been motivated by one sure thing all of these years: work. You went to work because if you didn't you would have lost your job, and if that happened you would not get a paycheck on a regular basis. Pretty compelling. Easy to see why you were driven.

Now you have to use your mind to motivate yourself to face the most mundane chores. You always knew you'd have all the time in the world to landscape your yard once you retired, or to finally put all those pictures in photo albums. (Yawn, scratch, snort.) So motivate yourself and do it. (After your nap, of course.)

> I have noticed that folks are generally about as happy as they have made up their minds to be.
>
> **Abraham Lincoln**

The control thing is a biggie. You may not think you had control because maybe you weren't anyone's boss. Not so fast. In a sense you had control over your daily routine because you *had* routine. And if you were in a power position, you may come down from that perch with a *splat*. Pick yourself up, wipe up your mess, and then get on with life. Read the chapter on spirituality for help…maybe even turn your power-thing into a servant's heart for others. Just a thought.

Lack of control means not being captain of your own ship. (A good thing, if you ask me…but of *course* you need enough control to wisely steward or oversee your life.) And lack of control may also mean something else. It may mean your lack of influence over the amount of income you have. Scary. No cute slogans here: just scary. This could put your mind in a tailspin. Here are some remedial actions:

- Take a deep breath and calm down.
- Reread the sections in this book (and other books) that deal with financial matters.
- Recognize that you are in a transitory part of life right now, and be prepared to make some changes, be they in your current lifestyle, in your physical address, or whether you are obliged to find part-time employment.
- Think. You have faced hardships in life, right? Hardships that brought you to your knees with worry and crippled you with fear. You are still here. You got through hardships, and life went on. That's the way of life—it manages to go on.

Reconnect

Because retirement is a transition that affects your whole person—spirit, soul, and body—now is the time to reestablish a few vital connections that are crucial to living well. Namely reconnect to yourself, to God, to creation, and to your community.

Reconnecting to You

You might fret so much about turning into a couch blob that you don't allow for necessary rest and contemplation. Constant activity can be a form of denial—too busy to think, you know!

While the couch thing is not the most auspicious start to a new life standard, let yourself lie there and look at the ceiling for a little soul-searching and serious thinking. Go visit those great cosmic questions you had as a teen.

When is the last time you have taken a personal inventory? When have you last wondered who you really are, what your purpose is in this life, or if you've become, in a sense, a stranger to God? (To God, we are never truly strangers. Strange, yes....) We will address your vital link to God in chapter 8. Right now, I want to ask you if you've become a stranger to yourself. Better yet, why don't *you* ask that question: *Have I been a stranger to myself?*

Have you been so focused on getting to this point in life that you've disconnected with your true self? This isn't New Age woo-woo babble.

You know as well as I do that life has a tendency to swallow us whole, and in the process we can lose our true identity. Chapter 3 dealt with loss of identity associated with work: Who are you, and what do you do? It also hinted at a deeper, more personal identity you may have left behind. What is the core you? What strong characteristics combine to make you who you are?

I had to stop a minute and ask myself these questions, and while I'm not certain how those who know me would respond to this, when I really and truly connected with myself, my positive response was this: I am, at heart, a kind person. (I'll reserve the negative response for a different time!) That is who Cynthia Yates is—a person who is naturally sensitive, kind, and hospitable. I cry when I see a Hallmark card commercial. The sweetness of it all is too much for my spirit to bear. I want to invite every stray dog I encounter to jump alongside me in the car and stick its head out the window. I want to bring smiles to the faces of the most marginalized people in our society. I want to feed people at a table that is groaning under the provision of God's grace and abundance. What about you?

Stump Time!

Write a paragraph about the core you. Really—regardless of how embarrassed you may feel by such outward manifestation of your positive traits and how hidden those traits may have been from yourself and from others.

Connecting to Creation

I decided a long time ago not to call it Mother Nature, Mother Earth, or even nature, for that matter, and I try to call it what it is— creation. Creation! How sorrowfully we have disconnected ourselves from God's magnificent world! And how sorrowfully, through the fall and through our neglect and abuse, has God's creation suffered.

A troubling disconnect between us and the natural world has occurred, and it is high time for us all to reconnect. We live within God's creation, which He called good. When we see God's hand in all

His works, we will develop greater reverence for all living things, and come to know Him more.

In Genesis we learn of our relation to our world. God ordered creation with humankind as its steward. As we become more acquainted with our environment, our responsibility becomes more apparent, and our worship of the inestimable great God who designed this world can only become more fervent.

Have you ever meditated on God's glory as you smelled the branch of a lilac, felt the strength of a tree, laughed at the antics of a sea lion, or watched birds play at the feeder? Just being outside for the sake of it (as opposed to making a mad dash from the parking lot to the mall) lifts the spirit and creates a feeling of pleasant play as we connect with creation around us.

Our prayers should be filled with thanksgiving for the wonder and complexity of our world, and with earnest intent to become the stewards we were told to be.

Here is an exercise: Plan to take a walk in a park after church on Sunday. Plan to make this walk a time of pilgrimage, of communion between you

> A man who understands the weather only in terms of golf is participating in a chronic public insanity that either he or his descendents will be bound to realize as suffering.
>
> **Wendell Berry**

and your holy God. Marvel at the grass, the bushes, the bugs, the flowers. Never forget that it is not the created order that merits our worship and praise, but the Creator, who is forever blessed. Remind yourself that in spite of the intricacy and beauty you see around you, *you* are created in His image, He calls *you* His child, and He misses *you* when you are apart from Him.

As with other exercises, there is a bonus or two with this:

1. You will develop greater tolerance and respect for all of God's creation.

2. You will become a better steward of your responsibility toward the rest of creation.

3. You will find profound joy in simple pleasures.

4. You will get outside. And off the couch.

Connecting to Community

Because marriage is the most significant relationship in our society, chapter 5 was dedicated to the impact retirement has upon wedded bliss. Retirement is also a good time for us to think about other relations within our community. By community, I mean the community of immediate family—in spite of distance—and the community of your neighborhood, town, and church, all of which may have fallen woefully into disrepair.

Family

How do you all get along? Great, so-so, or not so well?

Past histories, conflicting personalities, disappointments, tragedies...welcome to the family. It isn't easy when adult children marry others who are not compatible with your beliefs or with your customs. It isn't easy to have grandchildren who may look like they're going to spring a leak from all their body piercing and cause their goth makeup to smear in ghostly streaks all over their tattooed bodies. Or to have parents who are too feeble to button their shirts or to even remember who you are. Or to have brothers and sisters and cousins and friends dropping like flies. All of these hurtful aspects about our immediate relations are age-old, timeworn, and shared by all of humanity, whether in a suburb of Tokyo, in the bush of Australia, or in an igloo near the North Pole.

We respond with profound, deep joy to the positive aspects of family and close relations. A daughter is caught in the frenzy of her own life, yet she calls when she sees a handbag that reminded her of you. A grandchild graduates (finally!) from college and whispers, "Thanks, Gramps and Gram" in your good ear after the ceremony. A sister's handwriting has gotten shaky, yet she still manages to send you her updates on the family. A friend looks in your eyes as he or she says goodbye for the last time.

Do the positives outweigh the negatives? Usually. We would be foolish to act as if all relationships are created equal, because they are not. Many close relations are anything but, having ended in either a cold war or outright estrangement. To formulate opinion about any difficult relationship is not the purpose of this book. The purpose of this book is to help you to live well in retirement. You cannot live well in a vacuum or if you are estranged from those you love, especially if your heart aches. I'm merely asking that you think about unresolved issues.

At least one TV personality these days dishes sound advice. I've only seen his show a few times, but Dr. Phil McGraw seems pretty good on the draw. I heard him ask a battling couple, "Would you rather be right, or would you rather be happy?" Those can be mighty tough words, when "happy" means keeping your mouth shut and marching back into the dysfunctional mix you call your own, to love and to serve. Or when it means letting bygones be just that and wiping a slate that is filled with pain completely clean.

I cannot make trite statements about this issue. I figure it's one of those things you'll have to think about when you're sitting on your stump. Would you rather be right or happy? Certainly, if the dysfunction in your life is unhealthy, I doubt Dr. McGraw would have you march in with denial and a phony grin. But if the dysfunction in your family is more like delightful messiness, you might choose to be happy, as I do. For me, happiness is complete when I am in the midst of the somewhat dysfunctional mix. My family has sometimes caused me pain, but family is nonetheless necessary to me.

You may not feel the same as I do and remain completely satisfied to maintain a peaceful—and safe—distance from close relations.

Thinking about your relationship to family may be necessary for you in retirement if you aim to live well.

Stump Time!

Pray for the family member with whom you are estranged. Come on—Jesus said to.

Others

Another community is the community at large—your neighborhood. I will save this topic for chapter 8 because I feel that community cannot be separated from Christian practice. Let me say this for now: We should know each other, and we should integrate, not separate, from the fabric of our immediate communities. Ditto with church community.

Maintenance

Chapter 7 deals with the body, the physical aspect of living well in retirement. Yet while writing about the brain, I wanted to suggest a few things to help keep the brain healthy.

In particular, I suspect that most of us have a nagging terror that we will fall victim to Alzheimer's when we age. This is serious stuff.

As I am writing, I'm noticing the doomsday tenor of my message. The dedication page of this book records my husband's request for "a book that offers a little advice and a whole lot of comfort." Yet this book seems to be turning into one big wake-up call.

At times, the statistics I've encountered while doing research for this book have weighed me down. Such is the case when writing about Alzheimer's, a sensitive subject since one of my close friends is possibly dealing with this heartbreaking disease. Right now, some experts are predicting that Alzheimer's will be the top health concern of the twenty-first century.

Alzheimer's is a hard disease to treat, especially in later stages. You may feel invulnerable now, convincing yourself it's perfectly normal to forget where you parked the car, but let me offer a scenario.

> **F**ailing brain function is not normal—it is a sign of disease, injury, or neglect.
>
> **Dr. Vernon H. Mork**

The year is 2024. You are in your late seventies, and your body is slowing down. Matter of fact, both you and your spouse have had some serious health problems, and your agility, stamina, and strength have been sapped. As has your wallet. One of you gets Alzheimer's. Now what? This dilemma is faced daily in scores of homes across the world. Close relatives to Alzheimer's would include senile dementia and stroke. Very scary stuff.

While claims abound as to what may trigger this misfiring in our aging brains, we must pray God's mercy on those of us who have been so diagnosed and pray for curative measures that will lessen the grip of these illnesses. Fast.

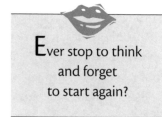

Ever stop to think and forget to start again?

Okay, Now Relax

There *are* other reasons why we forget where we parked. The consensus of doctors who specialize in such things is as follows:

- Our gradual decline in memory can begin as early as age 30.
- The longer you live, the more stuff your brain has to sort through when trying to retrieve information.
- We have lots of distractions and are stretched too thin to think straight at times.
- Slower reflexes may be the result of age-related slower speed of signal transmission.

Reactive or Proactive

I tend to think of conventional medicine as reactive rather than proactive. When you get *sick,* you go to your doctor. When something *hurts,* you go to your doctor. When you are *injured,* you go to your doctor. I don't know of anyone who takes the time and spends the money (aside from his or her annual physicals) to visit the doc to say, "Feeling terrific. Just thought I'd drop by."

I tend to think of, shall we say, *un*conventional medicine (alternative) as proactive. The "health nuts" have

It's not that our minds wander but that they may become less nimble than before at directing various circuits and brain functions toward a new target while keeping the previous target on hold.

Dana Book

been screaming at us for years to abandon our destructive eating habits and lifestyles in order to gain and maintain good health. Through the years I have found many of the claims from these *un*conventional sources to prove true.

While the conventional medical community requires correctly monitored tests and trials, anecdotal evidence to support natural healing methodologies is mounting. Several suggestions from the field of natural health offer a protocol for brain health:

- The aluminum issue. I've read dozens of times that the aluminum in cookware and antiperspirants is damaging to the brain. I have also read dozens of times that this is pure folly. For what it's worth, natural health care professionals recommend stainless steel cookware and aluminum-free antiperspirant.

- The mercury issue. Ditto. A loud cry has been coming from alternative practitioners for many years that mercury fillings in our teeth is destroying our health. Some predicted long ago that brain health would one day be mightily affected by mercury. (I do find it curious that as I write this, public health officials are recommending that pregnant or nursing mothers reduce their intake of certain fish for fear of too much mercury.) The American Dental Association has treated this claim as bogus and continues to insist that all that mercury in our mouths is safe—even after all these years. For what it's worth, natural health care professionals recommend removing the mercury from your mouth (with a dentist who knows the proper protocol).

- They also recommend that you have a good source of high quality essential fatty acids, such as fish oil.

- Veggies, veggies, and more veggies. (No, French fries and ketchup do not count.) Organic greens with a splash of unrefined virgin olive oil should be on everyone's plate every day.

• Walk, walk, and walk some more. Let your arms swing. Get out in the sunshine.

Use It or Lose It

You can exercise your brain in many ways:

- daily crosswords

- jigsaw puzzles

- needlework and knitting

- card games

- board games such as Scrabble or Backgammon

- computer games (if you are confident you won't become addicted)

- discussion groups (which will also keep you social)

- reading

- navigating a maze

- switching from your right hand to your left (or vice-versa) for simple tasks for a few minutes each day

- testing your debating skills

- memorizing a poem or a prayer

- dusting off the old clarinet and tooting—music invigorates your brain in many ways

- learning another language

> It makes sense that aerobic exercise should be good for the brain, because it's good for the cardiovascular system and that system is a gateway to the brain. Walking increases the brain's metabolic activity.
>
> **Robert E. Dustman, Ph.D.**

A simple method to help avoid forgetfulness is to write things down. Make lists, write all over your calendar, use address books and

> Do not conform any longer to the pattern of this world, but be transformed by the renewing of your mind. Then you will be able to test and approve what God's will is—his good, pleasing and perfect will.
>
> **Romans 12:2**

appointment books. I keep a separate address book with phone numbers of family and friends in the glove compartment of my car.

The Art of Memory

The art of memory, says Samuel Johnson, is the art of attention. I'll say.

Sometimes we just get plain lazy. Constant behavior patterns can lull us into effortless routine. As good as routine is, it is helpful to shake things up and add something different to each day.

Here are some exercises: Eat at a different table, sleep in your guest room, watch a different TV show, walk your favorite trail in reverse.

You can learn memory techniques, and books and techniques abound to help with this. These habits can help you maintain good memory:

- Get enough sleep and pay attention to natural, circadian rhythms (more on sleep in the next chapter).

- Eat wholesome foods and get enough protein.

- Wear protective helmets when engaging in sports and keep your head safe.

- Maintain optimal health through exercise.

- Control your stress.

- Stimulate your nervous system and your senses.

7

What's a Body to Do?

CYNTHIA:

It's like this—on those rare occasions when my health was of sufficient quality to support a hike in our glorious mountains, Joe would respond, "Give me a break—I hike in the mountains all week." In the scope of his career, Joe had gone through several pair of work boots, spent untold hours on snowshoes, and fought scores of forest fires with a Pulaski and a shovel. His body has been a tool as he hefted chain saws, cleared trails, and carried heavy backpacks. And while there is no question that Joe is my Wonder Man, he is not exactly Charles Atlas, a health nut, a gym bunny, or one of those lean, mean, jogging machines. Let me tell you a little about him.

Joe Yates wears his hair in the same style he has for decades (except now it's white and he has less of it), and after several years of my nagging, he's finally out of jeans and into khakis. Some of the time.

Joe would eat steak or hot dogs every night, and he thinks Coke and a pack of M&M's are the perfect lunch.

Though my husband likely believes Coca-Cola was invented just for him, he has responded favorably to my admonitions and avoids this drink. (Among other things, soda pop can be death to strong bones.)

Joseph takes sensible supplements when—and only when—I put them on the counter with our morning tonic, and he eats what I put in front of him. His exercise comes exclusively from laboring about our small farm and not from weight lifting or formal aerobics. He will join me for a walk if I ask. In other words, Joe takes care of his body because I take care of his body. During my absence, the supplements go untouched, hot dogs come home from the market, and his easy chair takes a direct hit.

Joe:

Boy oh boy, this is beginning to sound like Joe's rebuttal! (Maybe in the next book I'll write the first part and Cynthia can respond.)

I'm relatively healthy, and I don't expect my body to break unless I physically abuse it, but I have treated my body like a tool. Sounds like a real man, doesn't it? I do have certain expectations of my body, and I will admit that based on the care that I give it, it may not hold up to my expectations. So Cynthia is right—I do need to take better care of myself, and not just when my vitamins are being force-fed to me. I sure hope she let's me write first the next time.

Only You Can Prevent...

Here are the top five preventable diseases in America that have helped spike health care costs by a whopping $200 billion since 1987:

- heart disease
- pulmonary conditions

Yates' Morning Tonic

This is a cleansing drink to have upon arising and well before any other food or beverage. Into a high-powered blender such as a Vita-Mix, combine:

> 1 entire lemon, rind removed
> 1 half-inch medallion of fresh, peeled ginger
> maple syrup or stevia to taste
> 1 teaspoon powdered magnesium
> 16 ounces filtered water
> 3 ice cubes

Whir until liquefied into lemonade. Serve with one 1000 mg vitamin C tablet. Serves two.

- hypertension
- diabetes
- mental disorders[1]

An article in the *Washington Post* (August 25, 2004) emphasized that Americans invest more on health care than any other industrialized nation. This investment has not made us healthier. Quite the opposite. I quote the article:

> Instead of taking active approaches to prevent disease, most people believe health care is a "reactive" process in which people go to a doctor only when they are sick. That's regrettable, because most of the "top 15" illnesses could be prevented by taking simple and affordable measures.

This chapter on health is a critically important chapter if you want to live

Welcome to retirement! My gift to you is this question:

Over the next ten years, do you want to work at developing ill health or preventing disease?

Ryan M. Wigness

well in retirement. Be warned: This chapter will call you to accountability.

What Is Health?

Now that you have the time and freedom to "follow your feet," you need the health to do so. What is health? The very word *health* comes from an old English word for *hale,* meaning "whole." Health is more than just absence of disease. It includes...

- having a sensibly upbeat attitude
- having reasonably wholesome relationships with God, with family, with neighbors, and with creation
- movement
- nourishing your body with real food instead of fake food
- drinking lots of pure, filtered water
- sleeping through the night
- laughter
- engagement with the world
- learning and growing
- the wise use of leisure and art and music
- having a servant's heart (a heart like Jesus') toward everything and everyone around you
- maintaining some semblance of balance

What Isn't Health?

Needless to say, I have a few things for this list.

- a miserable attitude
- continuous, unchecked sinful behavior
- stress, depression, manipulation, addiction, or scorn
- isolation
- lethargy

- eating foods that have been concocted in a chemical plant on the Jersey Turnpike (As Dr. Joseph Mercola has commented, "Technology is great, but we sure don't need to be eating it!")

- swigging unlimited cups of coffee all day and never touching a water jug

> **A**ging is
> not a disease.

- insomnia

- candidacy for grump o' the year

- sitting around passing critical judgment on anything that does not buttress your own opinion

- a door shut tight on learning and exploration

- scorn for good literature or art

- day after day on the golf course or at the bridge table with nary a thought about the plight of others

- imbalance—probably our most common condition

Golf and Bridge Caveat

Please don't get too exasperated by my referral to golf and bridge. I'm using these pastimes as examples because they are common. (I would use curling and Old Maid if they were as common.) Though I haven't swung a club and do not know "two hearts" from "no trump," I am a fan of both of these pursuits.

Healthy Concerns

I have no doubt that when you bought this book you first turned to the chapter on finances, and then you zoomed straight to this chapter. Perhaps you are looking for answers, for a magic bullet, for some secret formula. Some of us are still looking for the fountain of youth! (At the very least, for some a way to restore the vigor of youth.)

The issue of health in retirement is positively enormous. Health is the determining factor in quality or quantity of life, and it affects us where we most fundamentally live. Health makes decisions for us.

Health keeps us up at night. Health spends our money, causes us to move close to our doctors, and separates us from active engagement with family, friends, church, and community. Health rules. Health dominates.

Health has become a gabillion-dollar enterprise as drug companies, hucksters, conventional and unconventional practitioners, researchers, supplement companies, New Age religions and philosophies, diet plans, and miracle cures all call to us: "Here's the answer, we can help, we can fix you, come our way." ("Give us your money" is more like it.)

> Earth has no sorrow that heaven cannot heal.
>
> **Thomas Moore**

It wasn't at all like this in our grandparent's generation, and I'll tell you why: First they lived, and then they died. We don't do that anymore. Our search for answers has become our life quest. We don't want to feel sick anymore or to even get sick. The character development we might experience while enduring weakness and the spiritual value of suffering or hardship aren't nearly as important to us as feeling good.

We have learned that comfort and ease have become our high-tech birthright. We may have forgotten to see the light of Christ in life's broken pieces. Or in the words of Paul,

> Praise be to the God and Father of our Lord Jesus Christ, the Father of compassion and the God of all comfort, who comforts us in all our troubles, so that we can comfort those in any trouble with the comfort we ourselves have received from God. For just as the sufferings of Christ flow over into our lives, so also through Christ our comfort overflows (2 Corinthians 1:3-5).

And so a new sentiment has entered our cultural reality: First you live, and then you get cancer, kidney stones, dementia, osteoporosis, arthritis, diabetes.... You go on an expensive treatment regimen and hope for a relatively tolerable existence.

Or first you live, and then you get hearing aids, trifocals, ortho-pedic insteps, Velcro-d tennis shoes, wide-brimmed hats, fake teeth....

(My sisters and I have echoed this comment so many times that it's entered our family's colloquial language: "Mom, do you have your glasses, your teeth, your hearing aid, your comfortable shoes…?"

None of us is far behind you, Mom.)

In spite of the fact that our predicted life span has been increased dramatically, we boomers are not the healthiest specimens walking the planet. My mother's generation seems to be somewhat more hale, and our grandparents', though shorter lived, seemed to have a higher quality of health. But us? Autoimmune diseases, chronic fatigue, true medical depression, adult attention deficit dis-order, impotence, prostate problems, a cancer for every body part…yet an-other list that goes on and on.

I have my suspicions as to what happened to our generation's bodies.

We grew up during the time that science became our sacred cow. Chem-icals and synthetics rocketed into our lives to make them easier. When I was little, cornflakes left in the cupboard for more than a few days would end up with worms. Now you can leave them

> Alcohol, drugs, cigarettes, lead, mercury, heavy metals, additives, dyes, hormones, pesticides, herbicides, fungicides, petrochemicals, exhausts, radiation....

in the box ad infinitum. And we think that is *good!* I remember pumping bug spray from a contraption until my head was in a cloud of DDT. I also remember city trucks driving down our streets spraying for caterpillars and mosquitoes. We rode our bikes through filmy droplets of white, misty goop that killed the nested caterpillars (and everything else in its path.) Chemicals. To make life easier. Wahoo.

Advances in technology brought radioactive, electrical, and mag-netic fields. There is no question that technology has brought much good. But we are bombarded by these fields from within and without our homes and cars.

Are We Truly Healthy?

I asked my Montana chiropractor, Ryan Wigness, to share thoughts about health. "Think of yourself as standing in a room with thousands of strangers in front of you, Ryan. What is the most important thing you want them to know?"

Many people are very confused about the difference between health and disease. They will go to the doctor to have their blood pressure checked, X-rays taken, and cholesterol screened. These are all good tests, but they test for disease. They do not check for wellness. When the tests come back "normal," patients assume they are healthy when in fact they may be on the way to creating a disease. High blood pressure, heart disease, and obesity are epidemic in this country, and they are a result of lack of wellness.

Here is the part that people do not want to hear: They are probably not healthy. It is time to wake up and realize where we are at. The good news is that we can still do something about it. If everybody would exercise 30 to 40 minutes three or four times per week, cut back on processed and fried foods, reduce refined sugars and flour, increase fruits and vegetables and dietary fiber, and drink 60 to 70 ounces of filtered water per day, we would be light-years ahead of where we are now.

If one of those fad diets seems too good to be true, it is. And don't be fooled into thinking that taking some magic pill will do the trick either. Weight Watchers is very helpful as is a book called *Sugar Busters*. The point is, don't fool yourself by thinking you are healthy if you are not, and *do something about it*.

Most people will agree with what I say and set the book down to pick up their soda and potato chips. Exercise and eating properly just takes a commitment, and if you are willing to make that commitment you will drastically lower your chance of disease. Don't wait until it's too late. As the proverb goes, "An ounce of prevention is worth a pound of cure."

Lest we forget pollution…the toxins we kids sucked through our lungs and through our largest organ (our skin) must have put everyone's liver on double time. We lived near factories and mines that flung sludge and waste into our water supply and sickened the air with poison. Chemicals, pollutants, and destructive fields have hammered us for so long that they've practically pushed their way into our DNA. Not to mention exhaust fumes.…

I plan on living forever. So far, so good.

Something else happened to us—or perhaps because of us. We became an automobile-dependent nation. The family car liberated us from our "dirty" cities as we fled to pristine suburban communities—not a corner grocer in sight. Few of us walk anyplace anymore. Yes, when I was a kid, my mom sent me on my bike or by foot to the corner store. We had corner stores back then. We walked. We biked. We gardened. We played outside. (Some retirees are moving back to urban environs. More on that in chapter 9.)

If there is such a thing as a stress meter (apart from that familiar blood pressure cuff), we boomers have caused its invention. We became upwardly mobile, pushing, grabbing, and getting more. We took on more work because the kids had to go to college. The kids cause stress, tuition causes stress, work causes stress. Guess what? Stress causes bad things to happen to our bodies.

We became distanced from each other, and our disconnection had a direct impact on our health. You better believe it! No backyard neighbors. No emotional safety nets. We now carry our burdens ourselves. Women once complained about their husbands to the sisterhood, a healthy consolation of commonality, as the repertoire of their annoyances made its usual rounds before they all headed home to make dinner for the bums. For the most part, men trusted other men to be there in a pinch, to lend a tool, to lend a hand, to provide the answers and skills we now seek at the home improvement store. Men talked about motors and saws and charcoal barbeques, happy to be the first on their block to have one. Relationships made life more secure, more stable, safer, healthier.

We don't move anymore, and we have little or no social capital. We also have become too distracted, busy, or lazy to properly care for our bodies. Add to this some people's genetic predisposition for certain illness. It's no wonder a lot of us are sick.

What is a wonder is that for the most part, medical science does not seem to have been too savvy about these factors. It seems to scratch its head, telling us our complaints are all in ours while happily dispensing pills for whatever ails us. And science—our sacred cow—still reigns, still holds most of us in its spell with its promise of a better tomorrow.

Get a Grip

You thought getting a grip on your *attitude* was important? Piece of cake. Getting a grip on the proper care, feeding, and stewardship of your body is one of the hardest things you will ever struggle with.

Sure, some intrepid souls our age and older have managed to get that grip and to hang on tightly. I'd venture that for the most of us, unless we have grown up with a lifestyle and worldview that centered around healthy habits, this will be a struggle to the end. It sure is for Wonder Man and me.

Just like many of you, we know what we are supposed to do to help our bodies to become more fit, and in the process, we hope, to make them more resilient to the toxic influences listed above. What do we do? In plain English, *we never stop trying.*

It's always Monday morning in the Yates' house—today we implement the newest plan, reinforce the latest push, commit to the brand-new resolve. Because of my books and research, I've been privy to more information than average person on average street. This can be troubling. I am often compelled to put us on some new bandwagon. But this information is also beneficial because we have been able to slowly but surely eliminate certain foods from our diets and to better understand the positive or negative effects of certain behavior, attitudes, and thoughts on our health. We are acutely aware of the importance of caring for our physical bodies. I should say, we are aware of how acutely important the care of our bodies is.

We can easily get into a pattern of try and fail, try and fail. If this is the case with you, I urge you to change your pattern to try and fail, try and try, try and succeed. As with brain health, *you simply must get proactive about your overall bodily health.* Too much is at stake: your future, the quality of your future, the quality of the future for your loved ones, and your finances. You could face insurmountable health bills from a medical expense you could have prevented had you gotten that "grip."

Stump Time!

You've answered so many questionnaires in the doctor's office that you should be good at this:

How old am I?

How many times have I been in the hospital?

How many times have those hospital visits been because of an accident?

How many times because of illnesses?

What kind of illnesses?

Could lifestyle modifications have possibly helped keep me out of the hospital?

What hurts in my body now?

What symptoms do I show?

For what have I been diagnosed?

Are there things I can do to mitigate against these health problems?

What is at stake if I don't do them?

Why don't I do them?

Will I give up?

Balancing Act

Just this morning (my fifty-seventh birthday) my 88-year-old mother lit into me:

"I don't know what's the matter with you. You're not getting any younger, you know, and you take on all these extra things. Now you have horses! Old horses! And sheep! Why are you doing this? You work harder than most farmers I know. (Like my mother knows any farmers.) You're going to kill yourself, Cynthia. You bring this all on yourself!"

Been there? I know. We're all always trying to balance our checkbook, our time, or our responsibilities. We shoulder too many responsibilities.

Life is a balancing act. At times it's balancing and juggling while standing on one foot in heavy hail and gale force winds with the hiccups. Our bodies are also constantly balancing and juggling and are fully dynamic. Our bodies cope with such things as outside irritants that include radiation and electric and magnetic bombardments. Our bodies work to balance noise, pollution, stress, and their own surging hormones. And while we sleep and rest, our bodies are actively restoring themselves.

Only when we become aware of this balancing act and join in as full-time partners will we find healthy equilibrium and wholeness. Dr. Andrew Weil says that "in balance there is stillness and beauty in the very midst of chaos."

Balance includes staying clear of "too much." Too much of anything—good or bad—will throw off your scales. Too much sun, too much cloudy weather, too much food, too much play, too much noise, too much rest, too much work.

Suppose you are a chocoholic. One day you realize, *Hey! I'm grown now. I can buy all the chocolate I want!* Which you do. Fill a whole cupboard with chocolate. What happens after the first lovefest between you and those mocha truffles? You slow way down. It was too much. Not good. Your body (vis-à-vis your appetite) knows this. If you stuff one more truffle into your mouth, you'll trigger a sit-down strike; if you can't control yourself, your body will make you uncomfortable enough to know you should. Balance. We should listen to our bodies.

As we juggle all the factors in our lives, we should take a cue from our friend the tightrope walker: If we lose our balance, we will go *splat.*

Medical Options

I am mystified that we cower in the presence of medical doctors and take their word as infallible. Sure, we may have nurtured trust through a long and beneficial doctor–patient relationship, but still....

Doctors are not God. They are fully human. Within their humanness can come errors in judgment or in diagnosis. You, the patient, are also fully human. Within your humanness can come such strong genetics that you defy all odds. Within your humanness may also come a body that—when balanced and given a fair chance—can begin to effect some of its own healing or do so in concert with medical care and prayer.

I am a proponent of both allopathic (conventional) medicine and alternative (unconventional) medicine. By *allopathic,* I am referring to the regular medical establishment. This medical establishment has been taking a lot of flak lately—because of soaring costs, malpractice claims, and countless testimonies of people who quit their medical docs and dove head-first into the swelling ocean of alternative therapies.

Beyond question, a few medical doctors seem arrogant, uncaring, and totally uninterested in anything other than their particular specialty or their opinion. "My way or the highway" could best describe these practitioners.

Some doctors simply do not listen to what we are saying, wave us off with the flick of a wrist, and send us packing with a prescription in our hands. Before we know it, we're in the parking lot wondering what just happened. (Except that we wrote a check for an office visit and now have a slip of paper in our hands.)

I am reminded of a term in a book by Dr. Sidney Baker—*meeching.* Dr. Baker tells us *meeching* is an old New England term for a look that pleads, "I am helpless, do me no harm." I'm guessing that many of us give our docs meeching looks.

Propaganda galore—some of it quite militant—beseeches us to abandon the drug pushers and to return to what once was conventional: folkloric, herbal, and "natural" remedies and cures. Watch it. This is a matter for ethicists to tackle, but for good or bad, our mortality rate is significantly lower these days due to medical advances, conventional medical treatment, and yes, drugs. The *quality* of our extended life remains another matter.

And now the flip side. I sincerely believe that most medical doctors and specialists are dedicated to our health and want only to serve us with their knowledge, experience, and good intent. *These doctors are busy.* I dare say we cannot remotely conceptualize the extent of their workload between patients, reports, hospital calls, and emergencies... not to mention that they are just like you and me, with family, friends, and personal obligations, one of which is to somehow find enough rest and relaxation to combat burnout. And along we come, indignantly stomping into their offices with the latest article from a health magazine and demanding "Read this." I mean, fair is fair.

Does the medical establishment have some serious "examining" to do of its own attitudes and presumptions? Yes. I have sometimes been bounced from doc to doc (as have you) and have heard a wide range of diagnoses for my health problems—diagnoses that in the end were questionable or downright wrong. I would like to make clear that the same thing has happened to me with alternative medical practitioners. (I remember one character who told me, "Oh, yeah, you've got cancer, but no problem, I can fix it by putting this vial on your chest." After which he disappeared into another room and I disappeared out the door.)

As with allopathic doctors, I have met a slew of alternative health care workers who are gifted, highly trained, and loaded with concern for my welfare. Because of a brother-in-law who is a chiropractor, I have had an inordinate amount of exposure to the field of chiropractic and have become a believer. Though I've read material that discounts chiropractic entirely or in part, I am compelled to say that feeling is believing. After many years of intermittent chiropractic treatment, I am becoming convinced that it should be part of every person's medical regimen. (But you must also see the physician of your choice.)

I have experienced firsthand the power of physical therapy, of massage, of herbal medicinals, of aromatherapy. I have also tried other modalities within the alternative scope that did not do a thing for me other than cost a lot of money.

My suggestion is that you consider integrating both allopathic and alternative methods of healing and that you remain extremely cautious of claims that sound too good to be true. (You know how the saying goes on *that* one!) Check with trusted friends, ask for references, and use your common sense. Good guys *and* charlatans come in all shapes and sizes and make claims one and all.

Should you integrate care, be utterly certain all of your doctors are aware of this and are apprised of any drugs, supplements, or herbs you are taking.

Does It Work?

True science rejects something called anecdotal evidence. In other words, without clinical, controlled study behind something (and you'd be surprised by how much the trials and statistics vary!), it is considered worthless and improbable. I'm not so sure I agree. If I had a friend who suffered from migraines for 40 years and then went to a chiropractor and *shazam!* migraines gone, I'd be tempted to consider that practitioner.

Could it all be in her head? It certainly was all *from* her head: the nausea, the pain that caused her to hit her head against the bed headboard, the debilitating effect that reduced her to lying in a darkened room, wishing she were dead. All in her head, alright. And to that I say so what? Please don't forget the mind-body-spirit connection.

When You Think Something's Wrong

If you think something's wrong, don't just sit there! Unlimited information is available in print, on the Internet (be careful of all kinds of crazy schemes and promises on the Internet), and from various health practitioners. Educate yourself. Start with this honest appraisal of any lack of action on your part so far:

I know I am going to have to finally deal with_____.
I figure I can still put it off for _____. After
all, I probably won't die until _____, and
anyway, I *will* get to this by _____. In the
meantime, I don't mind feeling like _____,
and no book is going to tell me how to live my life. After all,
it is my life.

When Something Does Go Wrong

If something happens that has the potential to derail you, I
encourage you to consider fighting back. Give your body all the care
it needs to heal, become proactive, and start your healing with a team.
Let me tell you what I mean.

In 1999 I was diagnosed with a bone tumor in my arm. The diagnosis came as a result of pain so intense I did not understand how
someone could bear such agony and not die. Conventional medical
wisdom was for me to go to a specialist in Seattle and have the tumor
surgically removed. My doc and friend, Pamela Roberts Oehrtman,
immediately sent me for second and third opinions. Pam is a rare breed
of doc and I am lucky (and sometimes surprised) that she puts up with
me. She agreed to be the conventional medical leg to a team I put together to help me try to beat the tumor. Pam would never have agreed if my condition was grave.

> **D**o you not know that your body is a temple of the Holy Spirit, who is in you, whom you have received from God? You are not your own; you were bought at a price. Therefore honor God with your body.
>
> 1 Corinthians 6:19

My team included Pam, a chiropractor, a physical therapist, my pastor, and a friend. Some of these people actually met to plan how they could work synergistically to help me help my body beat the tumor. This may sound like a lot of work—or downright goofy—but from my perspective it was vital. I was fighting back.

I gave it my all. My pastor prayed and counseled, my friend listened. The chiropractor and therapist adjusted and massaged and worked toward lessening my pain. Pam monitored every step. Reports made their way from one team member to another. In the end, the team didn't fail, but our attempt to avoid surgery did. Everyone stuck with me through painful postoperative therapy to gain back the use of my arm.

Of my team, some were paid professionals, some volunteers. Each person took his or her role seriously, and through our efforts no stone was left unturned. We had the sense to recognize that surgery was the answer.

> Typically,
> the five senses
> change as follows:
> - hearing—mid forties
> - vision—mid fifties
> - touch—mid fifties
> - taste—mid fifties
> - smell—mid seventies

Drugs

"My wife and I pay $300 a month and we simply can't afford to keep it up," says one letter writer. "Why are drugs so expensive?"

We pay more for drugs in America because we have no price controls on the gabillion-dollar drug empire. The drug companies insist they need their gabillions of dollars to further research.

The Food and Drug Administration claims that imported drugs are not safe because they could be outdated, contaminated, or counterfeit.

In a desperate attempt to save money by purchasing prescription drugs from out of the country—say, Canada—some people have been scammed by swindlers who set up websites and happily attract you by displaying a maple leaf or the Canadian flag.

In 2006, Medicare will begin to cover some prescription drug costs, but understanding the benefits takes a calculator, a GPS, and an advanced degree from Princeton.

> Understanding the impact of diabetes on people over age 50 is one of our new frontiers. [There has been a] rapid increase of people with diabetes in the past 11 years.
>
> **Robert J. Willis**
> *Director of the University of Michigan Health and Retirement Study*

Medical Problems to Be on the Watch For

In addition to the usual lineup of potential health problems such as cancer, heart disease, hypertension, arthritis, and diabetes, here are four other health issues you should be on guard for:

Osteoporosis

From a booklet on osteoporosis: "The truth is, many women don't know they have osteoporosis until they break a bone. In the United States, half of all women over 50 eventually develop a fracture as a result of osteoporosis."

The widespread availability of technology to measure bone density has made it possible to identify women who are at risk for osteoporosis long before fractures are imminent, according to the Harvard Women's Health Watch.

By the way, according to Dr. Clifford Rosen, premature gray hair is a predictor of low bone density. Guess what? I had premature gray hair and have low bone density.

Cataracts and Glaucoma

Annual eye exams are important. During our aging process, the protein in the lens of our eyes begins to get cloudy...this can lead to cataracts, which should be caught early. As should glaucoma. Glaucoma comes from pressure building inside our eyes. The pressure damages our optic nerve. This can lead to blindness. The big issue about glaucoma is that there are no symptoms. It can only be found through an eye examination. Stay on top of this one.

Dental Issues

Our dentist, Dr. Larry Clayton, has a few words for you:

"Teeth—ignore them and they'll go away. Literally.

"Which teeth should you brush and floss? Just the ones you want to keep. So goes conventional dental wisdom.

"Teeth are like a favorite old car. We enjoy and ignore them as long as they're working well. When they break down, they are a pain and can take a big bite out of the budget. Just as with the old car, regular, preventive maintenance can assure long, pleasurable service."

On life's highway, one of the stops that can assure a pleasant, healthy retirement is your dentist's office. Preventive dental examination and necessary maintenance should go hand in hand with proper nutrition. Comfortable, affordable, golden years are far more likely if you have a preretirement overhaul. Have a healthy journey!

Digestive Problems

I want to scream and throw things at the TV when I see all the ads for heartburn and indigestion! (The screaming comes from my long-standing practice of and belief in a more natural lifestyle.) Keep your guts clean! As we age we are five times more likely to be constipated, and we have lower amounts of acid in our stomachs, which leads the way to stomach upset and gastritis. Detox your body, look into probiotics (healthy bugs), get fiber inside of you, drink enough water to flush yourself clean, and exercise. (Like beating a drum, isn't it? Eat right and exercise—ya think there's a message here?)

Insomnia

Pam Oehrtman feels that sleep is underestimated and wanted to have her say. I am happy to share my doc with you:

> Twenty-one years of medical practice has taught me that many Americans have significant sleep problems. An inquiry into the sleep history is usually very revealing when I am seeing a patient with significant physical, emotional, or fatigue symptoms. Asking about the usual bedtimes, the time it takes to fall asleep, the number of awakenings for *any* reason (including rolling over, hearing noises, or adjusting the covers), total sleep time, early morning awakening, and the sense of alertness upon arising can be very helpful in determining if insomnia is an active issue. In my experience, *patients don't report and physicians don't ask* about sleep issues often enough. I wish all physicians would consider a sleep inventory as the fifth vital sign.
>
> Science tells us that what was once thought to be a very passive state is actually a time when our brains are very active. Restful sleep is a requisite for good health. Animal studies show us that sleep is necessary for survival. The life span of rats is shortened to 3 percent of normal when deprived of sleep. In humans, after 24 hours of

wakefulness, the metabolic rate of the brain decreases significantly, resulting in decreased body temperature, decreased immune system function (as measured by the white blood cell count), increased heart rate, irritability, decreased respiratory muscle strength, and decreased release of growth hormone.

In middle-aged adults, eight to ten hours of sleep is considered fully restorative. In our senior citizens, the time it takes to fall asleep and the number and duration of overnight awakenings increase, so the time spent in bed must increase as we age.

Sleep deprivation can occur in up to one-third of normal adults because of lifestyle choices. This has everything to do with the availability of the incandescent light bulb as well as the over-crowding of our schedules with music lessons, sporting events, good causes, and life at warp speed! Insufficient sleep can cause impaired short-term memory encoding, impaired attention (ADD-like symptoms), emotional changes (anxiety or depression symptoms), emotional liability, low energy, and decreased libido. Falling short of one or two hours of sleep per night over an extended period of time may lead to daytime sleepiness, irritability, attention lapses, decreased daytime performance, muscle aches, and depression. National Institute of Health data suggest those with chronic untreated insomnia are 40 times more likely to experience major depression, 25 times more likely to experience anxiety disorders, and 3 times more likely to become addicted to alcohol. This is very sobering data indeed.

The goal of people desiring optimal health should be to awaken feeling refreshed and move through the day feeling alert without effort, even when placed in a boring or monotonous situation. Evaluation of insomnia symptoms when they persist past three weeks and careful attention to health habits that promote sleep are essential steps toward a healthy lifestyle.

Food for Health

If you want to see me come alive, if you want to see my face glow, get me talking about the merits of real food to fuel and nurture our bodies. If you want to see me come unglued and to see my face darken, get me talking about what I consider the utter tragedy that has befallen

> The U.S. food industry is the remarkably successful result of twentieth-century trends that led from small farms to giant corporations, from a society that cooked at home to one that buys nearly half its meals prepared and consumed elsewhere, and from a diet based on "whole" foods grown locally to one based largely on foods that have been processed in some way and transported long distances.
>
> *Marion Nestle*

the United States' food supply. I rarely step inside a regular supermarket anymore. (If you want to know where I shop, you're going to have to spring for my last book, *Ditch the Diet and the Budget...and Find a Better Way to Live* [Harvest House].)

I cannot be shaken from my conviction that we should be consuming unadulterated food without sprays, pesticides, dyes, hydrogenated fats, preservatives, sugars, and "flavors." And I am not alone. As more of us become informed, I hope a groundswell clamor will reach the ears of the giant food industry. They will listen if enough of us squawk. In my opinion, we should eat veggies and fruits (preferably organic) and seeds and nuts and untreated meats and healthy fats and fresh eggs. In our home, we try to include a lot of green and a little protein at every meal. To us, anything else is window dressing.

I'm not certain, however, that many of us really give a hoot about our food source. This is unfortunate because our health (and therefore living well in retirement) is at stake. We simply refuse to change our eating habits.

"Wild salmon and broccoli for breakfast? Are you kidding? Everyone knows we're supposed to eat boxed cereal for breakfast. Or coffee and a roll. Get out of my face, lady. Who do you think you are?"

I'm just someone who has read and researched a ton in this area. I can only wonder if our blind acceptance of processed foods is in part due to the pleasant "mouth feel" and instant satisfaction most manufactured foods offer. It may also be due to the sin of gluttony, to our sincere lack of knowledge about the ingredients in and processing of foods that have been plied on us, and to our inability to truly grasp the responsibility we have toward our bodies. Go back and read what the apostle Paul had to say. You can find it in 1 Corinthians 6:19-20. For whatever reason, we seem to be unwilling to make healthy changes. Just like Dr. Wigness said, we put the book down and grab our soda and chips.

Stump Time!

Go to your pantry and find a box or a can of processed food. Read the ingredients.

Now read the ingredients on an apple.

Food Intolerance

A Chinese proverb goes like this: Whatsoever was the father of a disease, an ill diet was the mother.

In her book *Food: Your Miracle Medicine* (HarperTorch), Jean Carper writes, "To know the right food to eat—or not to eat—depending on your health circumstances, is to have an unprecedented wealth of knowledge with which to treat and prevent health problems, ranging from colds to cancer." She goes on to say, "There's also mounting evidence that certain foods have disastrous health consequences for a surprising number of people with unsuspected food intolerances or allergies."

> In my experience, the most common complaint shared by all [people with gluten or wheat intolerance] tends to be fatigue.
>
> Cynthia S. Rudert

I have a sense that "unsuspected food intolerances or allergies" are one reason many people are successful at weight loss and begin to feel good on the recent low-carb craze. (By the time this book is published, I can only wonder what the latest craze will be. I sincerely hope it is "low-consumption"...think *that* will catch on?) High-protein, low carbohydrate regimes eliminate certain foods from our diets—particularly highly refined wheat and gluten. I suspect that lots of people are unknowingly intolerant of wheat and gluten. In some cases, these people have a full-blown problem called celiac disease. (A tricky problem to diagnose, since it often presents itself first as an autoimmune disease.) Once those culprits are no longer eaten, the body feels a whole lot better and can get on with the business of being a healthy body. Dairy products cause havoc with some people who are unknowingly lactose intolerant.

> As many as one out of every 150 Americans lives with celiac disease, according to a study done at the University of Maryland School of Medicine.

Foods that my husband and I avoid (most of the time—we are not fanatic) include...

- hydrogenated or partially-hydrogenated fats: margarines and just about every snack food created by man
- refined oils—to us, this is a biggie. The only oils we allow in our house are cold-pressed virgin olive oil for salads and unrefined virgin coconut oil for cooking. (See the appendix for sources.)
- processed meats: hot dogs, lunch meat, bacon
- commercially raised meat and poultry
- sugar and artificial sweeteners
- sodas and juices (unless we juice our own in the Vita-Mix)

The Glycemic Index

I became interested in the glycemic index as a matter of personal curiosity. A book called *The New Glucose Revolution* (Marlowe & Company) taught me a lot. The four collaborative authors claim that the glycemic index shows us the natural way to eat. By following this index we eat nutrients in slow-release form to energize our body without putting strain on certain organs such as the pancreas.

What is it? The glycemic index ranks food from 0 to 100 to show whether a food will raise blood sugar levels fast, moderately, or slowly. Knowing which foods have a moderate or low glycemic number is valuable because our bodies can restore normal blood sugar levels better after absorbing a slowly digested food than after a quickly digested food. This information is of particular importance due to the skyrocketing incidence of diabetes in our country. (This is a book for people of retirement age, and many of us are grandparents. I'm concerned about what we are doing to our children when we feed them nutritionally barren foods or foods that spike their blood sugar levels.)

> Fast food has been one of the most unhealthful dietary developments in human history.
>
> Dr. Andrew Weil

High glycemic foods include processed foods that use refined flours. They also include sugar-laden beverages such as sodas and juices. Most breads, rice, pasta, and just about all potatoes in all their glorious forms rank high on the index. Carrots, while good for us, are mighty high on the glycemic index. If we eat carrots in our house, we are sure to eat them in combination with low glycemic food and only at dinnertime.

Some people may opt to avoid high glycemic foods altogether, some will incorporate high glycemic foods with low glycemic foods to balance, and some, like Joe and me, will try to eat high glycemic foods only later in the day. You may want to look into this matter for yourself.

> Stevia is an herb that is 300 times sweeter than sugar and packs zero calories. Widely used in Japan, stevia does not adversely affect blood sugar. A quarter of a teaspoon is equal to 1 teaspoon of sugar. Two tablespoons are equal to one cup of sugar.

Celebrate at Table

While most of us eat to ease hunger pangs or because "it is time to eat," others find immeasurable pleasure in growing, preparing, and serving wholesome food. Eating a meal is much more than consumption. Let's not trivialize the celebration of each meal. Food is God's provision to nourish our bodies, and a growing body of evidence shows that eating correctly is a life-or-death matter for our bodies. It most certainly is vital to living well.

The Importance of Water

The importance of water cannot be overstated. One naturopathic physician, Herb Joiner-Bey, considers dehydration to be a public health hazard, especially for those over 65. You must be vigilant to adequately hydrate yourself each day. This means pure, filtered water. For every cup of coffee or tea you drink, you should drink two cups of water. Drink pure water, and drink half your weight in ounces each day.

Incidentally, those in the know say if you wait to drink until you feel thirsty, you are already dehydrated.

> As we age, the already unreliable thirst sense gets even less sensitive. Nothing hydrates the body better than water.
>
> **Herb Joiner-Bey**

Move It or Lose It

As Pam says, "There is no pill I could prescribe as excellent as exercise."

You simply have got to move. The older you get, the less muscle tone you have and the creakier you get. Movement is health. You must be dynamic, not static. *This is not optional.*

The psychological, emotional, spiritual, and physical merits of movement are extraordinary. I needn't go into detail here—you know how well you feel after you've had a brisk walk in the bracing fall weather or after you've flailed about in water aerobics. You know how much better you sleep when your body has been physically active. You know how happy and content you are after a night of contra dancing, which brought you into close contact with several other people. And there's always golf....

Not wanting to marginalize the value of golf, I called my neighbor Harry.

"Harry, do you feel healthy after you've played a round of golf?"

"Not if I play like I did yesterday."

If we flip movement inside out, what do we find? What damaging effects does lack of exercise have on your body, besides probable weight issues and poor lung capacity? A book on aging from the editors of *Prevention* claims 250,000 deaths per year are the result of lack of regular exercise, as is an increased tendency toward heart disease, diabetes, cancer, and osteoporosis.

I am in shape.
Round is a shape.

Walking

Walkers show much greater mental alertness, less tension and stress, less fatigue, and more vigor. Walkers are better at golf, better at bridge, and are better in bed. Hello? Hello? Where did you go? Oh! You went out to find friends to start a walking club!

Here are some exercises to get you moving:

- Sing in the rain.
- Power walk the dog.
- Handcuff the grandkids to your waistband and explore the neighborhood.
- Turn an old broom handle into a walking stick.
- Bend over and pick up litter as you go.
- Stretch high to touch a fluttering leaf.
- Wade in the old mill stream.
- Ask yourself, *When is the last time I went outside to play?*
- Pledge to spend quality time outdoors every single day this week.

Some Suggestions to Keep Your Temple Spiffy

What do I mean by keeping your temple spiffy? *Shave.* In the chapter on marriage we ran into a fellow who was eager to retire so he could "let it all hang out." Watch out. This is a time of freedom and relaxation, but it is not a time to let yourself go. Here are some helpful reminders:

- Stand, sit, and walk erect. Pull in your bottom when you are upright.
- Don't go anyplace wrinkled.
- Wear clothes that fit—maybe a fraction too big for a leaner look.
- Don't hurt the heart of a holy God by wearing seductive clothes in public. (I can't believe I'm telling this to people our age.)
- Don't rest until you find the right hairstyle.
- Floss.
- Don't rub your eyes.

The Cost of Health

Economists analyzed the data from the University of Michigan Health and Retirement Study. A particular survey of the people over 70 determined whether chronic health problems led to "wealth depletion," that is, 10 percent or more loss of total wealth. They found that the wealth of single people was significantly affected by chronic health issuers. Married couples' wealth was often depleted by 10 percent or more when husbands developed a new health problem.

The cost of health is a doozy of a topic to try to get straight. The best I can do is to generalize and share insurance information that is current at this writing.

In 2000, 27 percent of older persons assessed their health as "fair to poor" (compared to 9 percent of all persons).

> Every day that you get up and walk under your own power is a great day.
>
> **Don Anderson**

Older African-Americans (41.6 percent) and older Hispanics (35.1 percent) were even more likely to rate their health as "fair to poor."[1]

As we boomers age, retire, and live longer, we will put an unprecedented strain on our medical system. So be patriotic! Keep yourself healthy!

Financing health care is a major concern to many retirees. Until the health insurance industry develops more affordable options, each one of us absolutely must stay up to date with our policies and review our health insurance coverage at least yearly.

Paying the Bill

Congress has attempted to narrow the gaps for people who suffer with expensive health care, but some pointers are still in order:

Under certain conditions, you can withdraw funds from your IRA, without penalty, for medical expenses. If you deduct medical expenses from your federal tax return, those costs that exceed 7.5 percent of your gross adjusted income can be funded from your IRA. Also, if you're unemployed for at least 12 weeks, you can withdraw from your IRA for health insurance premiums. You won't be penalized for premature withdrawal, but the money will be subject to tax.

> Paying all this money would be much easier to swallow if we received glowing health in return.
>
> Dr. Joseph Mercola

Small businesses (50 or fewer employees) and those who are self-employed can set up a medical savings account (MSA), which is linked to high-deductible catastrophic health insurance. The self-employed can deduct 100 percent of contributions to an MSA, which are tax and penalty free when withdrawn for IRS-defined medical expenses. At this writing, MSAs are in a somewhat experimental stage.

"Preexisting conditions" clauses are becoming limited or prohibited by law. After 12 months of coverage, no preexisting condition limit can be imposed on people who maintain their coverage, even if they change jobs or plans. Neither can a group discriminate against an employee or dependent based on health status.

The COBRA law provides that if you leave your job, you can remain in your group health plan—at your expense— for up to 18 months (three years for spouses and dependents facing a loss of employer-provided coverage due to an employee's death, divorce, or legal separation).

> **O**ne report from 1998 claimed up to 97 percent of all hospital bills are wrong.

Employee Benefits

Health insurance benefits will follow some retirees for life. There is usually an open period during which a retiree may choose to switch to a different policy under the aegis of the retirement benefit program. Benefit programs will continue until the retiree reaches Medicare age, when they automatically switch to "supplemental" coverage.

Conversion of Health Benefits to a Private Policy

Depending on medical benefits, some employees may be faced with purchasing their own coverage once they leave the benefit program of their employer through retirement. A guaranteed conversion period is covered by law. You are entitled to convert to a private policy at this time regardless of past history and insurability.

Medicare

Medicare covers a big chunk of your medical expenses after age 65, but its coverage has some gaps as big as an eight-lane expressway. Call the Medicare information hotline for coverage information: (800) 633-4227. You can reach the Medicare Rights Center at (212) 204-6229 or www.medicarerights.org.

Filling in the Gap

How do you pay for expenses when they are not covered by Medicare? You have three options, if you don't count paying out of your own pocket or turning to Medicaid (we'll talk more about that in a minute).

1. Purchase a supplemental policy through the retiree benefit program of your previous employer.

2. Purchase a Medicare HMO. This concept has had some hard times, but because of a recent change in Medicare law it seems to be picking up steam again. People debate the efficacy of joining a health maintenance organization, and one negative aspect is that you have to see the HMO's doctor of choice. Belonging to a Medicare HMO can be sensible in some parts of the country due to denser competition for your medical dollars. This option, however, is often passed by.

3. The old standby Medigap policy is usually the choice of retirees. Though premiums are starting to spike on these supplemental policies, shopping for good coverage with a good company at an affordable price is still possible. Gaps in Medicare coverage are covered only according to the terms and provisions of your policy.

Medigap Insurance

Unless you live in Wisconsin, Minnesota, or Massachusetts, which have their own plans, you can choose from ten standardized Medigap policies (creatively labeled A through J). Plan A is the most basic policy; plan J is the most advanced, with a premium to match. When considering a Medigap policy, shop. The difference in prices for the same plan from competing A-rated companies can be substantial.

Medigap policies are priced in three ways:

1. Attained age: Premiums increase as you get older.

2. Issue age: Premiums are based on your age when the policy is purchased and will not jump without an overall increase in premiums on a class-action basis.

3. Community rate: Premiums are based on geography. Everyone in the same area pays the same premium (some age restrictions and penalties are associated with this).

Long-Term Care

Should you buy long-term care insurance? This is a tough question to answer. There are valid reasons to consider this coverage (and the sooner the better; premiums are easier to swallow the younger you are). It is increasingly hard to rely on family members to care for you when you are old and infirm. Statistics already tell us that more than 30 percent of us will need long-term care, and a scary assortment of medical conditions require experienced and professional staff.

Will you be one who will need long-term care? If you do need this care, who will take care of you? Joe and I decided to eschew this coverage (saving a couple hundred dollars each month on premiums), and this was our reasoning:

If one of us gets ill, we are confident the other will provide care. This is risky. It can almost be considered a step in faith. For instance, will I be able to care for Joe if something happens when we are both 85?

Since Joe and I both believe that there are times when "heroic" measures interfere with our natural life rhythms, we are less inclined to consider advanced measures to maintain a life that just may be ready to go home to the Lord. Yet what if we "naturally" linger—and need care to do so? We know that our son and his wife will step into that gap if needed. This will certainty be a burden. Though I understand what most people mean when they say they "don't want to be a burden," I don't buy it. Neither does the Bible. Joe and I will care for ourselves as best we can and do everything we can to stay independent, but if the time comes that we need care, here we come, Joshua and Molly! Get our room ready! (You will read about our room in Chapter 9.)

You (or your adult children) may not agree with this sentiment. In that case, rest assured: Many long-term care policies are on the market today, and I'm suspecting many more will come. After all, 76 to 79 million of us is a whole lot of people...many of whom have not yet thought this through.

According to a GE Center for Financial Learning Survey in 2003, 13 percent of households have long-term care insurance. What do the other 87 percent plan to do?

- Fifty-one percent do not know.
- Two percent expect other family members to care for them.
- Eighteen percent expect Medicaid to care for them.
- Sixteen percent expect their spouse will care for them.

Medicaid

Medical bills can wipe you out—and wipe out any estate you want to leave your heirs. Look into a Medicaid Qualifying Trust, whereby you divest your assets into a trust and receive interest payments, thereby conserving assets to go to your heirs. You need to do this with good, sound legal advice, and recognize there is a long waiting period of a couple of years or more before it kicks in. A qualified estate lawyer is invaluable in this case.

Helping Your Parents with Their Estate Plan

Retired or not, many of us face the bewildering task of caring for our senior parents. Juggling our emotions is hard enough with the reality of physical and custodial care, but what to do about Mom's or Dad's dwindling bank account? In particular, nursing home costs are eating away at everything.

At this writing, Medicaid can still protect a portion of your parents' savings from overwhelming long-term health costs. Specifically, the law now allows parents to give a portion of their savings to children (or others). By giving away money, your parents might reduce assets enough to become eligible for Medicaid.

- Medicaid rules allow your parents to protect "exempt" assets (such as a home, household goods, a car, and prepaid funeral expenses). *Caution:* Check with the state where your parents reside for its rules.

- Medicaid allows the creation of specialized trusts to preserve assets.

- Medicaid allows you to purchase a Medicaid annuity or promissory note, which will help keep parents financially secure when one of them enters a nursing home.

- Medicare or Medicaid may pay for home health care and delay (or offset) the need for nursing home care.

- If your parents are no longer capable of making wise, responsible financial decisions, talk with them about a custodial trust account.

Custodial Trust Account

These accounts can be established with most banks. Under this arrangement, the person in control of the money in the account is not the person who owns the money. Examples would include parents who oversee an account for a minor child, or an adult child or friend who manages an account on behalf of an elderly person. But there is little to no accountability unless there is an audit or unless the custodian is court-appointed, so be aware that this responsibility can be abused.

8

The Spirit of Retirement

CYNTHIA:

I hold my husband's hand before each meal and share grace. I flop into bed exhausted, to hear his quiet but resolute voice pierce the dark: "Our Father, who art in heaven...." I sit with him most mornings to share Scripture, praise, and prayer. My husband's faith seems rock solid and strong.

I am bemused by the memory of the first time we decided to pray out loud together. We were seated on our bed in the middle of the day. Our legs straight out in front of us, our feet pointed upward, we looked like a couple of little kids. There was dead silence as we both stared into empty space. For whatever reason I do not know, we were too embarrassed to look at each other.

"You go first."

"No, you."

"No, you."

Kind of goofy for a married couple, especially for two people who were (and remain) on fire for the Lord. We were smitten, submitted, and sincere in our walk with Christ. But church? For Joe, church was always another matter. Maybe a faith "journey" seemed superfluous to Joe. After all, he already had "found" Christ.

Joe and I both acknowledge the importance of fellowship and of a church community. We both believe that we diminish the body of Christ when we stay away from church. And still, not a joiner by nature—and maybe a bit leery of the pratfalls of the church community—Joe would easily busy himself away from church on Sunday mornings. But just for so long. As time has passed, my husband has come to understand the value—indeed, the obedience—of church attendance.

JOE:

I just wish it were true—I may at times be a rock, but if you look closely you'll see fissures and cracks and a few chunks missing. I can easily justify "why not," being obedient to the "why" is much more difficult. Yet without the Lord in our life, there would be no life as we know it.

I don't perceive myself as devout as the man across the aisle, I don't extend my hand as readily as I should, and I don't go down to the coffee hour after church because I don't talk churchy things very well. You get the picture.

When I have extended my hand, drunk coffee, and found out that they don't all talk churchy, I was rewarded and honored to be in the company of folks just like me.

When men are not comfortable, they stand back with their hands in their pockets, a lot like they did the first day of school way back when. We are still kids at heart. But take your hands out of your pockets because you can't shake another's hand that way.

What's God Have to Do with Living Well in Retirement?

In chapter 2, I explained that living well has to do with living according to God's purpose for our lives. That is our driveshaft.

Throughout your work life you may have been driven by ambition, by appeals to your ego, by encouragement from others, by the hope for advancement, by the security you were creating for yourself.

Just the other day I happened upon Rick Warren's popular book *The Purpose-Driven Life.* (Okay, I bought it at a yard sale for a quarter.) While I have not had a chance to read this book, a glance at its table of contents suggests that it is a "must read." I particularly like one sub-title under a chapter entitled "You Were Planned for God's Pleasure." It reads, "What Makes God Smile?" I can tell you what makes God smile without reading what this man has to say: You do. Especially when you are living according to the purpose He has for your life.

Rick Warren says it, I say it, undoubtedly countless others say it: You have a purpose in life, a purpose greater than paying off the mortgage and sending the kids through school. A purpose greater than retiring your gift-edness from others and heading into the sunset in your golf cart. A purpose even beyond sharing your giftedness with others. That purpose boils down to your relationship with God.

> **A** casual acquaintance with God is not going to cut it.
>
> **Rev. Bill Baumgarten**

To exclude the spiritual from your retirement means you are going into this phase of your life on two-thirds power. Probably less than that if you factor in the abiding power of God the Holy Spirit when you have surrendered your will to Him.

The Disconnect

This chapter isn't all about God. It's about God and your spirit. Without question, God enters into this domain in a big way, but so does the notion of inner peace and, in a sense, smelling the roses. (Which, I might add, were put here for us to smell.)

Maybe you have turned a deaf ear to God for a long time. It's easy to do. At first a bit of a blush when Sunday mornings rolled around, a tinge of guilt, but in no time you were sleeping in or filling the Lord's day with work or play. Leisurely Sunday mornings with the paper became natural, and fellowship at church, a distant memory. Frankly, you were glad to be out of that place anyway, bunch of hypocrites! Given enough time you could find dozens of reasons to stay away from church, and each one has a name: Charlie, Jack, Fran, Susan....

And the Bible? Either on a bookshelf, in a box, or consigned to a yard sale years ago. There is enough proof in the world today to warrant ridding yourself of that book, enough arguments to give you the excuse you need to avoid it. Any sophisticated or educated person will tell you the Bible is a Judeo-Christian myth.

Look. I don't know about you, but I've had my moments. Moments when bombardment from the world has sent the tiniest sliver of doubt to prick my skin: How can I be so gullible? What makes me think the God of the Christian Bible is real and no others exist?

To live and to let live would be much easier. This all seems so unfair, so unreasonable...why, it sounds downright un-American! We're supposed to be a melting pot, a pluralistic society where everyone's belief system is accepted and no one has the right to call anyone's belief wrong. Worse yet, wrong enough to send anyone to hell.

Sure I've had those thoughts. How do I cope? I am cautious to not promote full-scale, 100 percent experience-driven faith, but I have come to believe that when I appropriate Jesus Christ in my life, I truly experience Christianity. In other words, my believing Christianity to be true does not make it true. It is true whether I believe it or not. But it is when I fully grasp the fact that I am a prisoner of the Lord—the One who summons me to lead a life worthy of my calling—I am better equipped to deflect the assertions of the world.

In addition to this appropriation of Christ in my life, in addition to the mountain of evidence that exists, from the historical to the archaeological to the prophetic, and in addition to the testimonies of people who have experienced the unfathomable peace and joy that comes from Christ, let me tell you what always brings me back to my base.

Someone like Mortimer Adler brings me back to my base. As America's foremost philosopher, Mortimer Adler was the chair of the Editorial Board of Encyclopedia Britannica and one of the founders of the Aspen Institute for Humanistic Studies. Mortimer Adler—a man who should have "known better"—became a Christian in his later years.

Someone like C.S. Lewis brings me back to my base. Like Mortimer Adler, Clive Staples Lewis—an unexcelled mind—went from atheistic tendencies in his early adulthood to becoming one of the leading Christian apologists of the twentieth century. C.S. Lewis, with a mind so exceptional that he could twist most experts into a pretzel and spit them out for breakfast, steadfastly clung to the cross of Christ.

The people in a church in Charlottesville, Virginia, bring me back to my base. Charlottesville is a place where Joe and I spend part of each year. There, in Thomas Jefferson's front yard; there, where the mighty University of Virginia rises from the ground with awesome presence; there, where the finest academics of the world come to speak, to teach, and to mingle; there, in a church where I meet men and women who look as if they do not need Jesus Christ but who fall unashamedly at His feet in submission to His will, I am brought to my base.

I will never forget one Easter morning when a man with world recognition and credentials as long as my arm, shook my hand—me, a stranger!—and beamed, "Alleluia! He is risen!" He is risen, indeed, my friend. And He stands at the door to your heart, waiting to shake your hand.

The Partial Connect

There is yet another variation to the argument against belief:

"I'm just not into religion. It's fine for those who need it, like it, or feel like they have to do it. I'll find my higher power my own way, in my own time. That's what this country is all about: You do your thing, I'll do mine."

I am averse to the expression *higher power*. That term came into our colloquial language long ago and stuck—someone's attempt to tap dance around his or her accountability to the sovereignty of the one true God. Lost you there, didn't I?

If God is real—and I believe He is—He must be huge. He must be a first-cause, end-all, colossal-beyond-our-limited-understanding Being unlike any other. If He is God, there can be no others. He is the only God, the one, true, unspeakable God who can squish you like a bug—but doesn't. A God who is not some sort of schizoid who changes His identity, the identity of His Son, or His means of salvation through space and time.

An uncomfortable proposition? You bet it is. Makes you squirm in your seat when you try to catch hold of its magnitude. (Stump session very much in order.)

Yet our discomfort with something, albeit metaphysical or spiritual, does not disqualify it as a truth claim. Nor do a bunch of whackos doing awful deeds in the name of *any* god, or a well-intentioned friend pestering you to death about your relationship to God.

Repeat after me: God. Not some higher power that does nothing, demands nothing, or changes in complete compliance to your whim and can be made in your image.

"Well, to me, God is…" we say with smug certainty.

"I don't believe a God of love would allow…" we reply as those who know.

Bear with some sass now as I grab hold of a popular axiom and push it your way. Who died and left you God? We seem to do all in our power to reinvent or recreate the one true God to make Him meet our terms, our notions, and our sensibilities. It's a wonder He doesn't squish us all.

God is wonderful, loving, and awesome, not some insipid, safe, nonthreatening "higher power." The fear of God is the beginning of wisdom, Psalms 111 and Proverbs 9 say.

Whoa! We're supposed to fear Him? Yes. High time we did, if you ask me. We are also supposed to thank Him. He has given us much to be thankful for and much with which to live well: creation, each other, artistic expression, Himself.

Where Were You?

It is hard for me to pick a favorite book of the Bible. If my back were against the wall, I'd choose Job. One of the poetic books, its depth of meaning and its metaphors and prose all blow me away. If Job is so awesome in translation, I can only wonder what it must be like in its original language!

In chapter 38, one gets the sense that God has about had it with Job's whining, and in a bit of that same "who died and left you God" sort of way, He says this:

> Who is this that darkens my counsel
>> with words without knowledge?
> Brace yourself like a man;
>> I will question you,
>> and you shall answer me.
>
> Where were you when I laid the earth's foundation?
>> Tell me, if you understand.
> Who marked off its dimensions? Surely you know!
>> Who stretched a measuring line across it?
> On what were its footings set,
>> or who laid its cornerstone—
> while the morning stars sang together
>> and all the angels shouted for joy?
>
> Who shut up the sea behind doors
>> when it burst forth from the womb,
> when I made the clouds its garment
>> and wrapped it in thick darkness,
> when I fixed limits for it
>> and set its doors and bars in place,
> when I said, "This far you may come and no farther;
>> here is where your proud waves halt"?
>
> Have you ever given orders to the morning,
>> or shown the dawn its place,
> that it might take the earth by the edges
>> and shake the wicked out of it?

It is hard to stop quoting from that astonishing book, and I urge you to continue reading on your own. But taking my cue from God, where were you when He laid the foundations of the earth? Want to know? You were already known, already planned, already set to be born in the twentieth century in the country, in the neighborhood, and on the street of your birth. A purpose for your life was already in place. If you think that is far-fetched, tell me this. Have you ever given orders to the morning?

Who Is This God?

So who or what is this God? God is a person, a spirit, invisible, alive. He is perfect, transcendent, and immanent. He is three in one, compassionate, eternal, faithful, and trustworthy. God is good, gracious, holy, impartial, and just. He is love. He is merciful, omnipotent, omnipresent, and omniscient. He is patient, long-suffering, and forbearing. God is righteous, self-existing, truthful, and unchangeable. God is sovereign and shows loving-kindness. And that's just for starters. (I told you He was huge.)

I'll also tell you what He is not: He is not a grump. A stern or grumpy God would not have given us butterflies or flowers that laugh in the breeze. Or hearts that sing. He would not have given us friends in time of need or the ability (indeed, the *mandate*) to be filled with His joy. He would not have given us His Son. Or Calvary.

A grumpy God would walk away from you and write you off because of what you've done. A grumpy God would have zapped King David flat when he danced before the ark. A grumpy God would have never, ever given us the assurance of His forgiveness and His mercy and His providence. The one true God—our *highest* power—is not a grump at all. Many years ago I wrote a piece that has gone unpublished. Maybe it was meant for this very chapter....

God Is Not a Grump

I may be a sinner saved by grace, but I am a sinner just the same, one who pesters the gates of heaven with annoying inconsistencies and defiance—*buzz buzz buzz*—and who worms her way into rather deep pits of distress. Yet in spite of my sinful nature and feeble compliance to His commands, He—the Almighty, the great I Am, God who is all powerful, all knowing, and all present—does not squish me like a bug.

This insight is so beyond my human capacity to grasp that it would take a host of angels—professor angels!—armed with scrolls, chalkboard, and rulers, to imprint this mind-boggling knowledge on my soul. Their angel eyes would no doubt be peering over spectacles in frustration at this stubborn bug, eyes filled with urgency and importance as angel mouths shout, "Think of it!"

Think of it! The God of the cosmos, the God of lightning and power, the God who cannot be defined or contained or limited to even the most profound human thought or human word, the God who called the world into place with a single command, does not squish those He loves. In spite of their failings.

> The LORD redeems his servants; no one will be condemned who takes refuge in him.
>
> **Psalm 34:22**

This is startling—that the Person who created and governs time and space, who orders physical and natural law, who knows all, would put up with my irritating buzz as it drones ever upward, sometimes stinging in its lack of charity and at least once drawing blood.

That a big finger does not appear from the sky and flick me off the skin of the planet and into orbit like a rocket on the Fourth of July is a perplexity. I would be gone for good, taking my irritating moan with me.

Why me? I want. I need. Pretty please with a cherry on top. How come?

On and on I whine when I want. I am silent when I fail. Empty space in place of endless pleas, I try to creep away. Yet there is no place I can go to hide from Him. I cannot fly fast or far enough to escape His stare. I cannot hide under a mountain of rocks.

I flutter my wings and arch my back in flight, soaring toward the free, open prairie of willful behavior, as far as the sky will take me. I sail and flap and sometimes land on forbidden fruit. He meets me there and pricks me gently with heart language: *No, no, my little bugette, this behavior is not pleasing to Me.*

At times I fly a full-force dare, teasing, taunting, defying Him with conduct that pokes—I grab a spear and run to gather speed and fly right at His heart. *Take that!* my sin says to the Powerful One, *and that!*

I sin. I am totally, miserably, and finally human. He is God. Totally, magnificently, and finally God. He could make it hard for me. Wings folded, I crawl into holes of despair, holes so black I cannot find myself. Yet He is there too. And He loves me. He picks me carefully from thorny tangle, my whine a whimper.

Hold me?

When I fold my wings and cry beyond the drone and beg for mercy at the throne, His finger could flick me away then too. But it doesn't. It guides and comforts. His hand becomes my hiding place, my protection from trouble. His scarred hand enfolds my broken body in a sheltering cocoon. I am utterly safe. Utterly loved.

> This is how God showed his love among us: He sent his one and only Son into the world that we might live through him. This is love: not that we loved God, but that he loved us and sent his Son as an atoning sacrifice for our sins.
>
> 1 John 4:9-10

Ours is not a God of wrath but of redemption. Once His enemy, often crash-landing from a dizzying spiral of evil behavior, we are shaken but spared. Our wings broken, He even bears our bruises. We are reconciled through His Son, holy and spotless. Providence. Mercy. Love. The God who is before all things, in whom all things hold together, pieces shattered lives together. Lives are made new, to fly on strong new wings in the free open space of grace. In spite of our failings. A grumpy God would have squished us long ago.

Stump Time!

Is what the world has led me to believe really true?

- that the Christian God is the cause of much prejudice and strife in the world
- that the Christian God is stern and unforgiving
- that the Christian God is myth

Maybe I need to investigate these claims.

- How could a God who gives us peace that passes understanding be responsible for strife?
- How could a God who became man and substituted Himself for all of humankind in a sacrificial death be unforgiving?
- Those mountains—and that baby, and that kangaroo, and the sun and stars—they really *are* gifts, aren't they? From whom?

The Source of Our Delight

God is the source of delight and joy. His Word and His work are our delight. We are commanded to rejoice. "Shout with joy to God, all the earth!" says Psalm 66:1.

We rejoice because God is present with us, because we find rest in Him, because we find comfort in Christ.

The Reconnect

How long since you've talked with Him? No, make that how long since you've *listened* to Him?

Someone once said that prayer is talking to God, and meditating is listening to Him. By meditating I don't mean staring at your navel and humming. I'm talking about meditating on the Word of God, spending time in silent reverence with only thoughts of His beneficence and glory. The very first psalm in the book of Psalms calls us to delight in the law of the Lord, and on His law to meditate day and night.

In his book *Prayer: Finding the Heart's True Home* (HarperSan-Francisco), Richard Foster writes this:

> In Meditative Prayer the Bible ceases to be a quotation dictionary and becomes instead "wonderful words of life" that lead us to the Word of Life. It differs even from the study of Scripture. Whereas the study of Scripture centers on exegesis, the meditation upon Scripture centers on internalizing and personalizing the passage. The written Word becomes a living word addressed to us.

There is more to listening than hearing. I often remind myself that good listeners listen all the way through. (A rough paraphrase of an injunction in Proverbs to keep our yaps shut as much as possible.) It is really important to hear what God has to say.

I am still somewhat nervous to open my heart to hear what God has to say to me. For one thing, though I intellectually recognize that I am flawed *(oh boy!)*, my personal nature is such that I am absolutely mortified and suffer profound embarrassment when I am found lacking. Because I will always be found lacking in the presence of perfection, I try to duck and maneuver my way away from any incoming messages. I get zinged anyway…usually when I am compelled to study His Word for writing projects. *(So, Cynthia…you're writing about forgiveness, are you? Hmmm.…)*

It is also important to listen more deeply for that still, small voice of God to thunder, to guide, to lead, and to distinguish false claims from truth. This is called discernment. Discerning the voice of God is so important that it is considered a spiritual gift.

One reason we may avoid listening at any level is that listening must lead to a choice to obey or to disobey what we have heard. This puts us in a predicament. Better to keep those earmuffs in place! And a good way to do that is to stay away from church.

Have you ever considered that when you stay away from church, you diminish the body of Christ? You also diminish your spirit by withholding it from the gospel and from the nourishment of fellowship.

The Fellowship of Believers

The Didache is a book that dates back to the turn of the first century. Many scholars consider it to be a continuation of the teaching of the apostles. I am holding a copy of the Didache on my lap right now and reading these words: "Assemble in great numbers, intent upon what concerns your souls. Surely, of no use will your lifelong faith be to you if you are not perfected at the end of time." Where did it say you would be perfected? Assembled in great members.

From the earliest time, we have been called to come together. We are certainly encouraged to find refuge from the crowds and cares of daily life, as did Jesus when He stole away to pray. But we are clearly told to come together in close-knit fellowship as the body of Christ. "Where two or three come together in my name," said Jesus, "there am I."

The early church set a standard for daily fellowship and active participation and friendship. It is worth noting that the unity of fellowship in the early church, according to J.R. McRoy, "was *not* based on uniformity of thought and practice, except where limits of immorality or rejection of the confession of Christ were involved."

There is more to church attendance than the fellowship of believers, and that is your fellowship with God. Beyond a doubt, you can commune with God on top of a mountain, in your garden, or even in your fishing boat. But when you partake of communion with Him in church, you experience a mystical union of fellowship that can only come from participating in the remembrance of the Lord's Supper. This is the banquet meal, a deep feast where we are fully family. It is a mighty commemoration of the covenant He has with us individually and with His church, the fellowship of believers.

> The body of Christ is diminished by your absence.

One last thing. We are to join in the fellowship of believers in order to be reminded *what* we believe. In the sermon, the Word of God—hello? *the Word of God*—is explained, brought to life, and used as a two-edged sword to bonk us over the heads, to remind us all who we are as children of light, to shame us, to bring us to contrition, to excite us, to bring us to tears of joy. And we complain if it goes over 20 minutes? Yet we can watch golf or baseball or mystery shows or soap operas until our bottoms fall asleep.

Stump Time!

Next time I hear a sermon I will...

- fall asleep
- let my mind wander and think about what I need to get at the grocery store
- become annoyed because the preacher is over the time limit
- listen

The Spiritual Importance of a Day of Rest

Those of us who take a shot at Sunday (or Saturday) worship often do so in a blur of activity and a white-knuckle commute. We race to church without thought of the clothes we wear, let alone of quiet meditation. This is not the way it was. There was a time when people observed a day of Sabbath rest...a divine command so important to us that the Law-Giver placed it ahead of filial responsibility and moral regard for others. "Remember the Sabbath day by keeping it holy," said the Lord our God (Exodus 20:8).

There was a time when we dressed in Sunday best and left the house with polished shoes. A time when we set ourselves apart from the week behind us, when we stopped to worship God, when we observed the Sabbath rest. A time when we recognized the divine imperative not so much to slow down but to stop. Stop to praise, stop to think, and stop to consecrate ourselves to the Lord. Stop to rest in Him.

The Sabbath principle, which most Christians practice on the Lord's Day, is one of God's greatest gifts to us. He used the very order of creation to establish and mandate that we pull away from push and shove, and meditate on Him.

Ask yourself, *Do I treat Sunday the same as any other day?*

Pledge to dedicate the Lord's Day to the Lord.

What Does God Want from You?

The way I see it, God wants three things from you:

First, He wants you to surrender to Him through His Son. This isn't just some tired old Christian salvation rhetoric; it's the way He set it up. A long time ago, I was ministering on the campus of the University of Montana in Missoula. An earnest freshman came up to me, hands wringing. "How can I know what to do with my life? How can I know God's will?" I mean, this kid was about to fall to pieces, angst all over his face. "Oh, that's easy," I replied, sending him into spasms of self-doubt and insecurity. "Just read the sixth chapter of the gospel of John."

Allow me: "The work of God is this: to believe in the one he has sent" (John 6:29). "For my Father's will is that everyone who looks to the Son and believes in him shall have eternal life" (John 6:40).

Though you were saved to do the works that God prepared in advance for you to do, your preeminent work is to believe in Jesus Christ. Pretty straightforward.

Second, He wants you to live a full, sanctified life. The subtitle to this could be "What Makes *You* Smile?" Do you think you would smile if you woke up every day feeling full and sanctified? Sanctified, by the way, means to be "holy and set apart." Set apart for Him.

Sanctification has nothing whatsoever to do with anything you have done. Nosiree. About the only thing you can "do" is to "believe in the one He has sent," because sanctification is 100 percent the result of the atoning sacrifice of Christ.

Third, He wants you to do the works that you were created in advance to do. I need to qualify this: Works have nothing to do with salvation. I'm not talking about salvation. I'm talking about servant-hood. Christ modeled servanthood constantly.

> You call me "Teacher" and "Lord," and rightly so, for that is
> what I am. Now that I, your Lord and Teacher, have washed
> your feet, you also should wash one another's feet. I have set
> you an example that you should do as I have done for you. I
> tell you the truth, no servant is greater than his master, nor is
> a messenger greater than the one who sent him. Now that you
> know these things, you will be blessed if you do them (John
> 13:13-17).

Stump Time!

What is the first thing you are going to say when you are in the presence of God in eternity? That is, if you're not sniveling under the floorboards of some puffy cloud, trembling in awe before the full glory of God. I've thought about this and know one thing for sure: When I meet Jesus in person I'm going to ask Him to hold me. Frankly, I can't wait. No fooling. What about you?

The Hereafter and Your Soul

Maybe you're not even sure you're going to be in the presence of God one day because you're not so sure about an afterlife. And what if you don't qualify?

There are some matters best left to people with other titles, and the deep and controversial issue of our souls and our spirits qualifies every theologian in the universe for serious stump time.

For sure, the Bible talks about soul and spirit repeatedly. An excellent book on this subject is called *Immortality: The Other Side of Death*, by Gary R. Habermas and J.P. Moreland (Thomas Nelson). Both men are highly accredited doctors of philosophy.

I searched this book for the meaning of *soul*, which the authors establish as not only real, but something that experiences immortality.

Habermas and Moreland make a strong case for the soul as they share evidence of life after death—something all of us will begin to think about sooner than later, especially as we enter retirement years. Are we just physical entities—body, brain, nervous system—or are we all of that plus mind and soul? The authors explain:

> If dualism [the existence of both matter and spirit] is true, then we are both bodies and souls. In this case, with the destruction of the former, it could be true that we continue to exist in a disembodied state indefinitely, or according to Christianity while waiting a new, resurrected body....
>
> Seeing is believing, and since the soul appears to be embarrassingly invisible, then we must remain agnostic about its existence. A slide of the brain can be made for an overhead projector, but a slide of the mind would be hard to come by.

The men then join "minds" to demolish any notions that life ends with physical death, and to insist that eternal life awaits us—one way or another.

Belief in the afterlife boils down to faith. People like Habermas and Moreland help us to appropriate some of the faith claims with a bit more confidence. If you wonder whether you *merit* eternal life—the heavenly version—let me tell you right now: You don't. None of us do. That is the good news of Christ. Go back to the Gospel of John: The work and will of God is for you to believe in the One whom He has sent—His Son, aka Jesus Christ. Incidentally, want to know who said those words in John? Jesus Himself. You know, God incarnate.

So what about your spirit? What is it, anyway?

In the *Evangelical Dictionary of Theology*, I find that "while…a person is thought of as body-soul, spirit is the special gift of God which places one in relationship to Him."

Ruah it is called in Hebrew, "breath of mouth" or "breath of wind." God breathed life into the first man: "The LORD God formed the man from the dust of the ground and breathed into his nostrils the breath of life, and the man became a living being" (Genesis 2:7). That, friend, is the beginning of relationship.

Into your hands I commit my spirit; redeem me, O LORD, the God of truth.

Psalm 31:5

The LORD is close to the brokenhearted and saves those who are crushed in spirit.

Psalm 34:18

Where can I go from your Spirit? Where can I flee from your presence?

Psalm 139:7

Our spirit is the seat of all of our inner dispositions: our reasoning, our decision-making, our courage, our understanding, and our attitude.

Ecclesiastes 12:7 tells us the spirit that was breathed into us by God returns to Him when we die: "And the dust returns to the ground it came from, and the spirit returns to God who gave it."

Our spirits are well, are complete, and are at peace when they are in right relationship with God, from whom our spirit comes, God who is spirit.

The psalmists (usually King David between a rock and a hard place) remind us that our spirit can suffer in this life. M.E. Osterhover says, "As the heights and depths of human existence are experienced, mankind's spirit is drawn to either God or the devil, [and] it receives blessing or the subtle influence of evil and ultimate condemnation."

For the record, yes, I believe the devil is real. So did Jesus, who actually preached more on hell than He did on heaven.

> Why is my language not clear to you? Because you are unable to hear what I say. You belong to your father, the devil, and you want to carry out your father's desire. He was a murderer from the beginning, not holding to the truth, for there is no truth in him. When he lies, he speaks his native language, for he is a liar and the father of lies. Yet because I tell the truth, you do not believe me! Can any of you prove me guilty of sin? If I am telling the truth, why don't you believe me? He who belongs to God hears what God says. The reason you do not hear is that you do not belong to God (John 8:43-47).

Spirit Boosters

How is your spirit these days? We've heard it, said it, and felt it: "Her/his spirits are a little down today." Perfectly human condition. What can we do to perk up this vital force in our lives? What do we do when we just feel blah? (I'm not associating this feeling to those of deep despair, pain, or suffering.)

I have ten suggestions. If your spirits are ebbing, maybe one of these will help.

1. Pray and meditate on God's Word. When you are down in the dumps, the last thing you feel like doing is taxing your brain to get un-dumpy. So just pray the psalms quoted earlier or others. Insert your name (or an issue that is bugging you).

2. Talk to a friend. Wonder Man certainly is my best friend in the sense that we have been together for decades, spend much of our time together, and know each other intimately. Yet there are times I need to take my deflated feelings to someone else. My friends Jo and Jan are good for me. We don't meet often, and it is not always to boost my spirits, but I can always count on either of them to join me at Brookies Cookies for coffee and to patiently listen while I sob out my heart.

3. Pick up your spiral notebook. Write a letter that will never get mailed, write a positively tragic poem, write a story, or just journal. Write on and on. Become the next Faulkner and don't use punctuation for a whole page...don't even come up for breath. Just write. (I guarantee if you read your creation a month or a year from now you will howl with laughter or blush with embarrassment.)

4. Along the same lines, do something artistic. Get in touch with the creative side of yourself and do a secret little one-person dance in the garage, sketch a still life, build a bird feeder, sing a song (do this to the golden

oldies radio station if you really want to get a lift), or shave the dog and create a new breed.

5. Speaking of dogs, spend time with your pets. Throw a Frisbee, groom a mare, pet a cat. Talk to them. Let them look you in the eye with those understanding eyes of theirs. At least you will know that *some*thing cares that you're in the dumps.

6. Take a walk. Don't walk down a long, dark, lonely street—walk in the company of others. Go downtown and window shop, walk to the bakery and buy hearty bread, or go to the club and walk on the treadmill. Place yourself in the midst of life.

7. Offer yourself in the service of others who are a whole lot more miserable than you. Visit someone—anyone!—in a nursing home, at the veterans' home, or in the hospital. Help in an elementary school. Walk puppies at the pound.

8. Eat. You heard me. Eat something wholesome that will nourish your body. You may very well be in the dumps because all you've had today was coffee and a sweet roll. (If this is true, don't tell me. I don't want to know—not after the last chapter.)

9. Rest. Dr. Oehrtman told us about the importance of sleep. Make yourself comfortable and take a snooze. Plan to wake up refreshed and raring to go.

10. Allow yourself to be a little blue every now and then. When the giggles and the smiles come back they will be all the more meaningful.

Inner Peace

What did the Prince of Peace have to say about this most important issue?

Peace I leave with you; my peace I give you. I do not give to you as the world gives. Do not let your hearts be troubled and do not be afraid (John 14:27).

I have told you these things, so that in me you may have peace. In this world you will have trouble. But take heart! I have overcome the world (John 16:33).

To be at peace means to be free from strife. The more spiritually advanced among us could say it is to be free from strife even in the midst of strife. Those dear Teflon-type people manage to keep a genuine calm and downright holy demeanor while the house burns down around them! Their trust in God is so powerful that nothing can rattle their cage, while the rest of us scatter like a fistful of BBs dropped on a slate floor.

Since I have always admired those who exhibit inner peace, I spent some time on my own stump reflecting this issue. I began with thoughts about any thing or behavior that destroys my chance at inner peace. Here is what I came up with. I have absolutely no peace...

- when some matter has been bugging me or causing serious interference in the quality of my life
- when some matter turns my every thought into obsession
- when I rehearse conversations with "offending" parties until I have them memorized as well as I do the Pledge of Allegiance
- when I am overcome with bothersome or negative emotions that include rejection or anger

But I'm the one who is supposed to know better, right? I write books, appear on TV and radio—why, I tell the whole world how they are supposed to live well under any circumstance. Author, read thyself!

All of my angst over an issue does not mean I wasn't slighted, hurt, misunderstood, gossiped about, treated poorly. That's not quite my point. My point is that *I do not have inner peace because of my angst.*

I taped a slogan to my computer monitor, and I haven't a clue who first said it, but the words are powerful:

"Someone once said that staying angry is like taking poison and waiting for the other person to die."

Who wants to swallow poison? Not me! And so I pray specifically about the issue affronting me or for the people involved. I'm a bit petulant about this because I know the drill: If I ask God to take the burden from me, He'll say, *Alrighty then, give it to Me.*

And I'll say, "I don't *want* to give it to you because then I won't get justice, I won't get my name cleared, and the record won't get set straight."

So He'll say, *Alrighty then, so enjoy the poison.*

And I'll say, "Okay! You can have it. As a matter of fact, take it, please. I do not want to feel this way anymore."

And He'll say, *Alrighty then.*

And inner peace will start to work its way into my spirit.

Outer Peace: Peacefulness with Others

The longer I live, the more convinced I am that our highest goal in life should be to be good neighbors.

When we were an agrarian society, we spent a good deal of time outside. Outside equated with community. As we've progressed through technology, we have barricaded our backyard door and become inside folk. And with the comfort of air-conditioned, upscale cars, we even stay inside when we are outside. Now instead of walking to a neighbor's for a spot of tea, we drive through an espresso stand. We have become homebodies and have feathered our nests with wall-to-wall carpeting and Barcaloungers. No other people are to be found.

I worry that meaningful contact between ourselves and others has suffered from lack of obligation to neighborliness. As I've written so many times, we aren't connected to each other anymore. At one time, the fellowship of believers mitigated against this ill, yet I wonder if the dizzying array of denominational differences and rifts have not added to our "estrangement by type."

Community is a critical component to the quality of your life in retirement. It is also a critical duty for you to nurture community throughout your retirement. To live well within our circumstance is a critical witness to a watching and needy world.

People often speak of peace with a sincere conviction to end war and strife, and well they should. I feel, however, that we would do well to recognize the truth behind such hackneyed slogans as "peace begins with you." It really should be "peace begins with community." It is hard to revile someone for whom you pray, or to try to kill someone with whom you break bread.

We are no longer civil. Let it become our legacy, the legacy of 76 to 79 million people, many of whom once marched for peace and protested war, to restore civility and community to a battered world.

> The world defines success in terms of what a person possesses, controls, or accomplishes. God defines success in terms of faithful obedience to his will. The world asks, "What results have you achieved?" God asks, "Were you faithful to my ways?"
>
> **Ken Sande**

If you are a Christian, you have a redemptive message: the love of the cross of Christ. When conflict arises—and it surely will, for conflict cannot be separated from relationships or from community—let the watching world witness the love of Christ.

Stump Time!

When in the throes of conflict or adversity, do I stop to ask myself...

- Who is the Christian in this equation?
- If it is I, do I follow Christ's teaching?

9

What to Do and
When and Where to Do It

CYNTHIA:

This is a good time for the rest of the story.

Early on the morning after Joe's retirement party, we began that fateful trip east for the winter to live as a blended and extended family with our son, his wife, and our two young grandchildren. Throw into the mix two Labrador retrievers, two cats, and two entire household moves during our first two months in Virginia. Oh, yeah…Joe was trying to jump-start his postretirement career, and I was in the midst of media tours for *Living Well on One Income* and writing *Ditch the Diet and the Budget*. Did I mention that we were bickering?

Let me add some more perspective.

We live in a 3400-square-foot home on ten acres in Montana. In Virginia, we moved into a 120-square-foot room with a clothes closet no bigger than a minute. Into this room we brought the equivalent of two portable offices, our winter clothes, and our 90-pound dog, Jill. Beside the drastic difference in space, our environment changed from mountain country to inner city, and the nighttime serenade of coyotes gave way to the boom of rap music from passing cars.

Let there be no doubt—Joseph and I have made a conscious choice to be ever-present advocates for our son and his family. That said, our move to Virginia so immediately after Joe's retirement was not the smartest thing we've ever done. We did too much too soon, and the stress from the circumstance nearly did us in. As I wax eloquently in *Ditch the Diet and the Budget*, life happened. Nobody planned for our transition to be hard, nobody bore responsibility for the fact that it was hard—it just happened that way. Joe retired. Josh and Molly moved twice. I had tours and a contract.

Besides, we were all determined to do our part to make our living arrangements thrive. What could be so hard? I'd already spent months at a time visiting our son's family. This would merely be an extension of that experience. Joe and I never accounted for our need for space.

Space! We needed all kinds of space! Space to be a couple, space to be apart, space to stretch out, space to kick back, space to sort things out, and for Joe, space to move from being a significant player in a spot where he'd been for 37 years to being a full-time husband, father, and grandfather. He wasn't even in the West anymore, driving down familiar roads. This was Jefferson's Virginia. Khakis were mandatory.

A year has passed since Joe's retirement. We are back in Montana for now. He busies himself around the farm, continues to establish himself in his new job, rarely sleeps in, and has finally gone fishing. (You should hear about the one that got away!)

Joe:

Well, Cynthia and I survived—to grow again, to be happy, and to be us. Would I recommend doing it that way again? *No!* But rather than the worse for wear, we are stronger.

Take it from me: Don't transition through too many major steps at the same time. If you retire, stop and smell the roses close to home—not all the flowers in ten states. And don't burn too much daylight.

God bless,
Joe

You Are Here—Now What?

I have brought you into our story to help you to conceptualize—or perhaps to rethink—your own retirement. I hope you've taxed your brain, peeked into your wallet, taken hold of your emotions, and recognized the importance and the purpose of living well.

And now you've arrived (or are putting such plans in place). No more deadlines, no more 6:00 A.M. alarm clock, no more 8:00 A.M. train. No more cold, dreary commute home. You are here. Now what?

Time Flies

In *Ditch the Diet and the Budget,* I addressed the issue of our time-stressed environments, be they at home, at play, or at work. Several other authors have written books that tackle time management. Yet we continue to wail that time has become our mortal enemy. I hit the brakes on that one. Although your schedule may be enough to choke a full-grown Clydesdale, you needn't panic. Time control is very much a matter of perspective.

I do not regard time as an enemy but as part of God's perfectly created order. The hours in the day, the morning and the nighttime, the seasons of the year—He created them all to help us to order our lives. Time is a gift. Managing time is part of our God-given stewardship responsibility. Managing your time is one step you can take toward living well.

Yet we've said it a thousand times: Time flies.

Time begins to fly when you hit the responsibilities of adulthood, and it is on the back of a booster rocket by the time you hit midlife. Retirement may present a chance to slow down a bit. This is a time to think about what to do with all of your time. I hope you will wisely use it to God's glory. I hope you will greet each day with a heavenward bow and a bold step into a life that is lived well.

Many of us waste a shocking amount of time each day. (In case you failed to get this gist by now, I do not believe the wise use of leisure and rest and play to be a waste.) These are some areas in which I see time wasted:

- poor stewardship of time during our daily routines
- lack of skills (or lack of interest to learn skills) that will abet wise time management
- crowded highways, intersections, commuter systems
- crowded stores and long checkout lines
- technology (like being put on hold by an automated phone system—argh!)
- other people's inability to manage time
- Endless vacuous TV, Internet, and computer game activity. According to Ken Dychtwald, who has authored books on aging, in 2003 the average retiree watched 43 hours of TV each week.

An Important Skill

A sensible way to manage your time effectively is by using a list. A list is a plan. It makes sense to write down what you plan to do each day. (It really makes sense if you have trouble forgetting why you walked from one room to the next!)

Many people use a wall calendar for appointments or birthday reminders or for upcoming social functions. That is a good system. It pays to record such things. But I am talking about lists for day-to-day activities.

Oh, man…now she wants me to write a list every morning? I don't even know what I'm going to do today! That's my point! If you haven't a clue what to do, your time may be poorly managed.

I am suggesting a list for those of you who have difficulty with time management. It's actually a sensible concept.

Wonder Man and I have been writing daily lists for years. We usually discuss the next day the night before (everything requires a balanced approach…the operative word here is *usually*). We list chores we'd *like* to accomplish, chores that *must* be accomplished, phone calls that have to be made, shopping or appointments that need to be tended to (shopping has its own list), bills that must be paid, obligations that must be met. For instance, if we have company coming the next day, we think through what we will serve and make a list of things to do and get. Our lists often evolve from ongoing conversation, and sometimes we write them on the run.

Time-Sensitive Matters

Two unwritten rules associated with list making are (1) once something goes on a list it stays on the list (moving daily from list to list to list) until it can be crossed off, and (2) time-sensitive issues are prioritized with an asterisk. In other words, if something positively must be accomplished in a given day, it is preeminent on the list. Here's an example:

I am drafting this section on Wednesday, July 14, as Joe is flying home from a trip out of state. We have company tonight. I am going to share the list I wrote for today. (Comments in parentheses are for your edification and were not in the original.)

Wednesday

- *swamp toilets (company coming, after all)
- fix sheep pen (this will take, like, *two minutes,* but it is one of those things that keeps getting put off)

- *draft chapter 9
- *meal plans and setup (we are eating outside in the shade of our home at 7:00 tonight)
- stepping stones (I've been having difficulty getting to the bird bath in our wildflower garden without stepping on the flowers, and the bath needs cleaning regularly)
- sheets and towels (clean sheets: Wonder Man is coming home!)
- check all gardens and the strawberries (to be sure they are getting enough water)
- *water A.M. (having a heat wave in Montana—lawn needs early watering)
- biscotti (was going to make gluten-free biscotti, but…nah)

Right now the sheep pen, the biscotti, and the stepping stones will more than likely find their way onto tomorrow's list.

Always try to make your meals celebratory.

Since company is coming, and we are dining al fresco, and I am writing a book, and Wonder Man isn't here to help, dinner is going to be an old stand-by: antipasto. I have an additional list, reminding me of tasks connected to the meal:

- cold drinks in ceramic tub
- bread, olive oil, and olives
- salami and mozzarella, basil and tomato salad, cuke—tall spears
- polenta
- cold broccoli pasta
- mixed beans with herbs
- dessert: lemon balm custard (made yesterday) with whipped cream
- strawberries—pick from garden
- decaf

Protecting Our Time

While not marching in lockstep to an actual blow-by-blow, minute-by-minute schedule, you should guard your time. When two people are in the house, early morning chores are easier and take half as long. One delight of retirement is to enjoy breakfast together. Since time is precious to us (after all, we don't know how long we'll be around), prioritize any particular block of daytime that you find special.

One daily ritual that Joe and I deem important is morning prayer. We have scheduled morning prayer for 9:00 a.m. daily. (Incidentally, I recently heard a radio personality say that the divorce rate among Christians is as high as that of non-Christians. Old news, right? The person went on to say that the divorce rate of people who regularly pray together was in the single digits!) Joe and I take turns leading the other in our morning prayer time, and we have come to regard this part of our day as essential. That means we make an effort to protect the 9:00 a.m. hour. We think twice before we obligate ourselves for any early morning appointment or obligations. (But if you want to save time, schedule yourself for the first doctor's appointments of the day.) Morning prayer calls for an asterisk because it is time sensitive.

Incidentally, we also try to protect Saturday morning. Throughout the history of our marriage, Saturday morning has been associated with delight. Just the sound of that word—*Saturday*—evokes good feelings. Joseph and I turn Saturday into adventure (yard sales), pleasure (a visit to Brookies Cookies), or indulgence (staying in bed and drinking coffee or tea on a cold winter morning).

None of these time management solutions are given to suggest you carry a clipboard or tie a whistle around your neck. But consider writing a daily list to glance at from time to time. Nancy K. Schlossberg advises retirees to keep a time diary to see how and where they spend their time. This will help them determine if they need more structure.

Unless you are married to someone like me who always has a project up her sleeve, it's fair to say that daily household chores and maintenance (after a time) will be on the short list. So what do you *do* with your time?

Vocation

Throughout this book, one message has come to you in many forms: The Bible knows nothing of retirement as a time to quit work and become self-absorbed. Pleasure and enjoyment are part of our human experience and most definitely part of a life lived well, but they should never become our purpose for living. Self-interest should not be put before the message of the gospel.

> **vo·ca·tion** \vō-'kä-shən\ : a divine call to God's service or to the Christian life; a function or station to which one is called by God

Our biblical mandate is to bear the image of God to a broken world. That is our fundamental purpose. I hope by now you have spent enough time on your stump to determine how that greater purpose translates to your individual gifts and vocation. When we use our talents, we are offering a living sacrifice to the Lord.

Think of it! What an impact we could have if our boomer generation led the march into the future with servants' hearts and a willingness to be Christians to a hurting world. This is an exciting time to be rid of the duty of our careers and to transform our selves, our marriages, our families, and our communities. (Your health or financial status need not hold you back. You can pray and intercede on behalf of others, or you can offer time instead of money.)

> **W**e can't retire from vocation!
> Rev. Mary Leach

The 10 Percent Principle

God tells us in Malachi to just try to out give Him. I fear that this verse is often used to bribe us to give to God what is justly His. "If you tithe you will reap a ton in return," some folks proclaim. Just maybe we skewer that biblical imperative from Malachi so that our tithe becomes something that benefits us. It is not about us. It's not a magic formula—tithe 10 percent so you'll get back heaps of money.

I fear too that we may think we're really doing well because we try to tithe 10 percent. (A little prideful, eh?) It's all God's anyway, folks. Churches and missions and youth groups and pastoral counsel do not run on thin air. We have a financial responsibility to all of this. Some Christians do not believe that the tithe is New Testament theology and that since it appears in the Old Testament, the 10 percent injunction was meant for the Israelites. To them I say, alright! Don't limit your giving to 10 percent—give more!

But have we ever thought about a different kind of tithe? Like time?

Joe and I plan to tithe at least 10 percent of our retirement time to the specific service of others. We don't feel this lets us off the hook 90 percent of the time. This merely causes us to focus our efforts constructively. In a 24-hour day, 10 percent of our waking time (factoring out sleep) is equivalent to around 1.5 hours. In a 30-day month, 10 percent is equivalent to roughly 1.75 days. In a 12-month year, 10 percent of our time is equivalent to about three weeks. This goal is ambitious, yet should the day come that we are fully retired from work, it doesn't sound so bad at all. Why, we could become volunteers! Volunteerism is intricately tied to vocation when vocation is broadly regarded as Christian witness.

Stump Time!

Where can I dedicate some percentage of my time?

Volunteer

If I can state one thing as a fact, it is that the unincorporated village of Bigfork, Montana, runs on volunteer power. Our volunteers are shepherded by other volunteers who have shouldered the responsibility of staging the many and varied events our charming burg offers. (It's no longer a wide spot in the road.) From an outdoor concert series, to decorating our town with thousands (it seems like millions) of colorful holiday lights, to parades, to food pantries, to the art center, to school advocacy...the list goes on. Look in our local paper, the *Lakeshore Country Journal,* and the cluster of smiling volunteers smiling back from pictures has pretty much one thing in common: retirement.

Remember that fellow Henri Nouwen from chapter 6? Let me tell you a little about him:

Henri Nouwen was a man who wrote more than 30 books and taught at Yale and Harvard. He was held in high esteem and could have called the shots for his retirement years, a life of ease and prominence at his fingertips. Yet this was a man who really "got" what Christ meant when He told us to be fishers of men and servers of others. Henri Nouwen spent his last years caring for a severely handicapped man, a man who by much of today's mind-set might have been "better off" if left to die at birth. To quote from Nouwen's book *Here and Now* (Crossroad General Interest):

> The compassionate life is the life of downward mobility! In a society in which upward mobility is the norm, downward mobility is not only discouraged but even considered unwise, unhealthy, or downright stupid....This is the way of downward mobility, the descending way of Jesus.

Where can you volunteer? Go outside on a clear night and look up at the stars. See how many there are? *At least* that many organizations, nonprofits, causes, events, and people need your involvement. How many of these causes could function without the steady presence of their volunteer force? Just this morning I read a classified ad asking for volunteers to help at the SPCA.

We tend to be quick to volunteer for a cause we believe in and support. Many causes are less in vogue than saving the dolphins or hugging a tree. (You know by now I'm a gung-ho conservationist.) Lots of agencies, nonprofits, and church and community sponsored groups serve the disenfranchised, the poor, the mentally challenged, and to be sure, the elderly retired with limited incomes or poor health.

Organized battalions of retired executives, professionals, or edu-
cators are happy to mentor the less experienced.

Volunteerism is alive and well in the world today, and when you are
retired you are in a position to be part of this critical aid. The appendix
offers a short list of volunteer options. Remember, our highest aim in
life might just be to be a good neighbor. Speaking of neighbors…

Where Are You Going to Retire To?

It may make sense to stay where you are for a short time. Transition from certain routine to uncharted life is enough change to carry
you for a while, unless alternate housing is already in place, or unless
you're setting off on the trip of your dreams. As my husband suc-
cinctly puts it, "Tell them not to do everything in one big gulp."

Also, relocation initially means loss of social capital—church,
friends, and sometimes family. For instance, I really like Virginia but
haven't had time enough to find and establish friends there. This creates loneliness for me. Though I may not have time in Montana to meet
regularly with friends, I know they are close, I see their cars in familiar
places, I wave, I call. I have social exchange with merchants who know
me. If you stay in your own home, at least for the short term, you can
find the bathroom in the dark, sit in your favorite chair to read the
paper, and sleep in the comfortable groove of your own bed.

Once the disruption of retirement has passed, you should be
grounded enough to think more clearly about where you want to hang
your hat. The primary geographic factors seem to be low-cost living,
health care, quality of life, and safety. Of interest is a recent trend of
retirees to move into inner cities and to move northward. Some magazines are dedicated to where you might live. For now I'd like to discuss your housing options.

Your Existing Home

You may own the deed. It's all yours. You know the rhythms of life
well in this old place, ride the seasons like a champion surfer, and
know the quirks of every neighbor on the block. The house will keep
you happily occupied for the rest of your life: the yard care, the

painting, the maintenance, the cleaning. The taxes, insurance, utilities, and upkeep. The new roof. Sorting (or planning to sort) through the collection of stuff—stuff everywhere, a lifetime of stuff. But it is home. It is Christmas in front of the stone fireplace, twinkle lights ablaze, and mistletoe hung in the same place every year for so long that the tack pricks have made a hole in your ceiling.

A Different Home

A different home: You may still have a mortgage on your home or decide it is too expensive to maintain. Or your home may be too big or too small. Your neighborhood may have changed in ways disagreeable or you may be tired of shoveling snow and want a warmer clime. You may just want a fresh start. But you don't want a landlord or a list of rules. And you want home equity.

There are advantages to sticking with home ownership, the chief among them having the freedom to do as you please—subject to zoning regulations or covenants. There is a sense of satisfaction and a sense of place that comes with home ownership.

It is common for retirees to scale down and move to newer, easier digs. Attractions include ease of cleaning, work-free landscaping, and one-level living to eliminate stairs. Besides moving to another locale for year-round climate comfort, retirees move to be near family (usually grandchildren), recreational areas (often golf), or to be closer to medical treatment centers. Hospital compounds now seem to be skirted by ever-growing housing developments that are inhabited primarily by the senior set.

A Second Home

The expense of maintaining a second home must be calculated far beyond its purchase price. Beside the obvious property tax, insurance, maintenance, and repair, you must now add the expense of security for both homes when you are away. Plant or pet care, surveillance, snow removal, and utilities do not stop because you are gone. This can be a financial burden.

What about your mail? Where will you vote? Where will you pay income taxes? Where will you be buried? How will your estate be taxed?

Traveling as we do to Virginia for extended periods has been costly in spite of the fact that we live rent-free while there.

Some mobile home parks have older models for sale that are inexpensive. You pay a monthly fee to the park, and you've escaped the high cost of living in and heating your home in the cold north. If this is your choice for a second home, be sure to drain your pipes and fill them with nontoxic antifreeze before you leave your primary residence.

An Adult Community

This is usually a recently developed suburban housing complex that offers homes designed with the retiree in mind. The minimum age is often 55. Children are allowed as visitors, not as residents. Housing costs depend on how upscale the complex is. These places frequently come with amenities for which you contribute dues: hot tubs, pools, exercise commons, parks, game rooms, a clubhouse, tennis courts, and walking trails.

A Foreign Home

Places in Mexico and Central America (Costa Rica in particular) hold allure to some retirees. Entire communities of expats have sprung up in such places, creating their own conclaves for safety and socialization. Because of significantly lower costs and the dollar exchange, some people claim that life in such places is fairly Edenic. "You can retire with not one but two domestic servants!" the ads boast.

A Condo

This is carefree living and home ownership all in one. You pay a monthly fee to cover your share of usual maintenance and yard care. You may only have to shovel snow off the stoop of your front door (if that). Everything is done for you. In exchange for this you have the life of Riley—and immediate neighbors, no pets (or small pets only), homeowner association meetings, dues, additional assessments for big maintenance expense, and strict covenants. ("What do you *mean* I can't drape my beach towel over my railing?")

A Mobile Home, Modular, or Double-Wide

Mobile home retirement parks are common in such states as Florida and Arizona. Usually the mobile home is owned by the home-owner outright, and rent is paid for the space on which it rests. These parks are often walled and gated for the security of their inhabitants. Parks usually offer a plethora of social activities, such as exercise classes, organized dances, crafts, and outings.

A Community Home

More and more retirees are living together in one home as community. This makes living affordable and provides safety, care, and socialization. It can also lead to heartburn if you end up with the wrong roommates. Siblings often live together in later years. Open communication and respect for house rules, as well as clearly defined financial participation, is critical.

A Rental

Some people were never in a position to own a home. Some people just don't want to be burdened by the expense, maintenance, or pre-dictability of life in the old homestead. They sell, liquidate as much as they can as they pare down to bare necessities, and fly the coop. An apartment or duplex or cottage is all they want. The costs associated with renting your residence should be weighed. I don't always agree that you are "pouring money down the drain" if you rent. In some cases, the cost benefit to renting (especially when it jibes with your new lifestyle choices) can be more financially efficient than owner-ship. For those who have no choice but to rent due to income restric-tions, a federal program is in place called the Housing Choice Voucher Program. It offers rental assistance to low-income families, the dis-abled, and seniors who qualify. Check with your local housing agency to find out if you qualify for rental assistance.

An RV

And then there are those who are born for the road. The house is sold, the few important heirlooms are put in storage, a mail-forwarding service is employed, a pair of folding chairs are bungeed to the back of the trailer, fifth wheel, or motor home, and away they go. These folks often eventually settle in a home, condo, or rental in an area they have found to be their personal mecca.

Living as Extended Family

I'm going to camp on this for a while and revisit a sentiment I've already shared in this book: We need to reconnect generationally. Call it my ethnic background, or call it growing up in the closed society of a moderately happy and occasionally functional Polish family. My early years in Schenectady, New York, *meant* family—drop bys when relatives would end up at our kitchen table eating cold cuts and rye bread and drinking coffee with my mom, weekends at some aunt and uncle's house, playing past dark with cousins, and holidays. It never entered our minds to not all be together. I could say the same thing for my Italian friends. This was my culture, my reality. This was all I knew. Then I moved to Montana. And then our kid grew up and moved away. Everything else seemed to go away too.

My two sisters are hundreds of miles from me, as is Mom. At times I feel adrift. I want the old days, not just for my own comfort or because of some unrealistic nostalgia, but because I believe they were better. Healthier. Dysfunctions and all. Yet we can't go back.

Life is no longer as simple as rooting ourselves in tradition. We cannot fall back on prescribed solutions, proclaim a matter settled (that's the way my father did it, and it was good enough for him), and expect all our decisions to follow in a neat row. The plurality of options in our world—real or imagined—has pushed the normative aside and caused us all to make choices. We see this clearly in traditional roles. For instance, when the normative held its grip, it was easy to know what it meant to be a man or a woman. All our choices were deliberate and set. Now—real or imagined—we have to make conscious choices about our role, about our place, about family.

If we continue to cling to past sensibilities without thought, we run into the risk of false security. Once again, I believe the old days were better in this regard. But we live in the new days. It is time to reclaim the day through thoughtful biblical imperative and to establish renewed social and cultural sensibility.

It is also time to reclaim the family. By that I am not entering the fray about definition of family—that too is for people of other titles. I'm speaking of generational integration and the layers of love and security that can only come from close relations.

Will our grandchildren grow up reminiscing about Uncle Frank and how he turned off his hearing aid when Aunt Irene was angry at him? About Aunt Clara, with those fluffy slippers that she carried everywhere, and her many medical emergencies? About Babci (Grandma), who rocked in a creaky rocking chair that gave background music to her Polish prayers? I'm not so sure.

I'm not so certain they will grow with fond recollection of backdoor neighbors who were gossips and stuck their noses in our simmering dinner pots, or headlights in the driveway causing a mad dash to hide newspapers under couch cushions and to fling clothes into closets. (Sometimes to realize it is merely a car turning around!)

While I despair about our grandchildren, I also despair about us. I feel this is nuts.

Joe and I make every attempt to see our son and his family year-round. It's not a matter of grandchildren knowing who we are, not a matter of sticking our nose in their stew pot. It's a matter of being part of a rich tapestry of functional and dysfunctional people called family. At the end of the day, for the grandkids, it will be about continuity and memory.

To live as an extended family in an adult child's house takes team effort. Sacrifices to independence, privacy, and space are significant. So is the value of modeling Christian community to the grandchildren and to a watching world. Needless to say, open and considerate communication is essential. If you consider this living arrangement either for part of the year or as a permanent residence, enter into it as a probationary enterprise and evaluate your situation after a designated period of time.

Many retirees live with adult children, especially as the parents reach their upper years. Though it takes all the fruit of the Holy Spirit to make this model a success, this living arrangement during your golden years can be worth its weight in gold.

Travel

What do you plan to do when you retire?

Oh, finish some chores around the house, do a little fishing, and travel.

The allure of the open road. The mystery of going down roads never traveled. The excitement (and even the disappointment) of finding the end of the road. Travel rejuvenates us. Opportunities for senior travel abound, and a few travel organizations are mentioned in the appendix to whet your appetite.

> Every so often, I need something to astonish me.
>
> **Mark Bricklin**

Many of us have an irresistible urge to travel. Whether to drive through the nation or cruise through the Northwest Alaskan corridor, we are explorers at heart (and maybe part nomad to boot). We can't sit still. Now that we're no longer tied to our jobs, we relish the notion of freedom to come and go, so go we do.

Travel conjures thoughts of endless possibilities: by foot, by horse, by car, by train, by plane. On a cruise, a safari, an eco trek, or an educational or cultural exchange. On a mission. Through a travel agent with passport in hand or on your own with no destination in mind. The world, the country of your dreams (or ethnic origin), the United States, your state, your city, your neighborhood. From your easy chair to a mad dash at O'Hare, travel beckons most of us to adventure.

A whole lot of us want that adventure to be comfortable. (We don't seem to be too eager to sleep on a rock pile in a sleeping bag just to know we can still do it.)

Recreational Vehicles

Many a dream about retirement has centered around a recreational vehicle. It is way at the top of the list: the motor home, the fifth wheel, the camper, the trailer, the conversion van. It is probably one of the most sought-after lifestyles after retirement—get an RV and head out for adventure.

Whether this story is part of the fabric of rural myth remains a question, but there is a well-worn fable here about a wheat farmer from Eastern Montana who retired. Sold his land. Money to burn. Bought him a big, fancy motor home with every new gadget under the sun. He and Ma hit the open roads of the prairie. First day out, the fellow put the motor home on cruise control and headed into the back to put up a pot of coffee.

He who dies with the most toys is nonetheless dead.

Though not yet equipped with automatic pilot, RVs come with lots of creature comforts. They can have small but full kitchens, bathtubs, washers and driers, slide-out rooms for more space, and hookups for Internet and cable. With the push of a button they level themselves, they have attached awnings, and some have the capacity for outdoor showers. And they aren't cheap.

While the romance of travel and the fulfillment of a dream may trump the downside of owning a recreational vehicle, you should consider the expenses and limitations.

- Expense of the rig, new or used. If used, is it in need of costly repair? How many miles has it seen? Are they highway miles or off-road miles?

- cost of insurance, license plates, and tax

- cost of maintenance, gasoline, and *storage* when not in use

- cost of dumping waste and park fees

- Your comfort. Can you live in a small (very small) space for an extended period? Will you be comfortable with the bathroom facilities? Will you mind driving or towing something the size of New Jersey and perhaps towing a car behind *that*? (Do you think all interstate traffic is created equal? Ever drive through Chicago during rush hour? Have you ever driven through Chicago anytime?)

After you factor the cost, consider how you intend to use your RV. Do you come out way ahead of the game by eating at restaurants and staying at motels for that trip to the Grand Canyon? (Especially if you travel off-season—a perk of retirement.)

Tour Your Town

Take what Joe and I call a local jaunt. We've learned that we don't have to travel far to see and experience new things, and frankly we have come to enjoy our nearby adventures even a bit more. We have no dirty laundry to unpack, we sleep in our own beds, and we haven't tired ourselves out. Here is what we do.

- Visit the chambers of commerce from local towns and gather interesting brochures for ideas.
- Read the local newspapers—especially the entertainment sections.
- Read and study tour books that cover our part of the state.
- Study maps (this is fun!) and try to find roads we've never driven. Sometimes we set out from our driveway just to find a road we've never traveled locally. Sometimes we set out just to get lost!
- Pay close attention to fraternal, church, or benevolent organizations when they post their bazaars, potlucks, or harvest dinners.
- We brainstorm to come up with a list of local businesses, art centers, and state or federal parks where we could take a tour or a stroll or sit through a lecture.

Elderhostel

Elderhostel is a nonprofit organization that provides exceptional learning adventures to nearly 200,000 older adults each year. Elderhostel offers over 10,000 programs in more than 90 countries. With the world as their classroom, this organization believes that learning is a lifelong pursuit that opens minds and enriches lives. (If I ever become unteachable, just throw dirt over me.)

Information on how to contact Elderhostel is in the appendix.

Education

We've all read about them in the newspapers: the 93-year-old who finally got her GED, the 80-year-old who went through college and graduated cum laude, or the 60-year-old who graduated from seminary after a career as a veterinary surgeon. Along with our information age comes endless opportunity to advance our knowledge in just about anything. Whether you are interested in a hobby, general knowledge, or a degree, with the aid of a computer you're off and running.

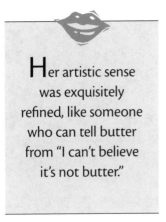

Her artistic sense was exquisitely refined, like someone who can tell butter from "I can't believe it's not butter."

University towns are popular destinations for retirement living, and not just for the intellectual stimulation and free lectures. Retirees are returning to school for that coveted degree or merely to audit classes for a small fee (or for free).

The Third Age and the University of the Third Age

The third age is the age of active retirement, coming after the age of youth and the age of work and homemaking.

A visit to www.U3A will bring you to the University of the Third Age. The Third Age University has no academic requirements for membership and no exams. It is a worldwide self-help organization that promotes learning for personal enjoyment and satisfaction. This extensive network offers information and help with issues ranging from health to employment to dating. There are links to Third Age Universities from St. Louis to Helsinki to Slovenia to Brisbane.

The City Library

Libraries are troves of fun and information. I urge you to designate specific library times. Visit regularly to read periodicals and to rediscover reading as recreation. Borrow books on tape, music tapes and

CDs, and videos or DVDs. Some libraries lend small appliances and tools and offer legal aid. Library bulletin boards are positively crammed with announcements of club meetings, lectures, or films.

If you live within walking distance of a library, visit each morning to read the paper. As a bonus…

> To be sure, music still matters to us. It's just that we have forgotten how to sing.
>
> **Andy Crouch**

- You will save subscription costs.
- You will walk.
- You will socialize by virtue of being out of the house.

The Arts

God makes the world with colors, and He makes us with eyes to see colors and hearts to delight in certain configurations of them. So, the visual arts. He makes a world in which movement makes sound, and gives us ears and brains to perceive and distinguish among sounds, and voices with which to make sounds. He creates us as beings living in time, so we experience rhythm and duration and tempo. Thus, music, as a joyous ramification of our being and of our being in this world.

Ken Myers

A Few Things to Do

- Don't forget the arts! Visit museums, read your own poetry at a poet's gathering, attend concerts, go to the ballet. The arts enrich our lives immeasurably.

- Start a book club. You started a walking club in chapter 7, so turn it into a walking-talking club while you discuss a book you're all reading. (Maybe this book.)

- Do something for family posterity: Write a cookbook of family recipes, paint a work of art, or write your memoirs.

- Write a résumé and apply to yourself for a job.

- Learn how to knit. Finally.

- Teach someone to read. Teach *many* someones to read!

- Turn yourself into an athlete by becoming active in a specific sport. I just read of an 84-year-old who *pole-vaults* for fun!

- Buy the *Off the Beaten Path* book for your state (Globe Pequot Press).

- Play the piano. The purpose of a piano is not to be a shelf for family pictures.

Happy Trails

Remember Roy Rogers and Dale Evans? They are two people who reminded us to sing, closing their weekly show with smiles as blazing as their six guns. And what did they sing? "Happy trails to you...."

Roy and Dale would then dig their spurs into Trigger and Buttercup and gallop off into the unknown, off into adventure, off into the certain call of duty and goodwill.

You are either setting off on the trail to retirement or have been on this trail for some time already. I have tried to clear the trail for you by removing rocks where you might stub your toe. I've erected signs to caution you of dangers in your way and to highlight the wonders you can expect to see. I've even built a few benches along your way so you can rest a while.

My wish for you is that your retirement is purposeful, that it is filled with contentment, that it is enhanced by the fruit of the Holy Spirit, and that it is Godward. I wish you lingering breakfasts with your loved ones, brisk walks in the fall, and peace. I wish for you to fully engage in your retirement years and to live those years very well.

Soli Deo Gloria

Appendix

This appendix is filled with specific information about organizations of interest to retirees and lists some sources for products mentioned in this book. Information about each listing is taken directly from its website.

General Information on Aging and Retirement
AARP
American Association of Retired Persons
601 E Street NW
Washington DC 20049
(800) 424-3410
TTY (887) 434-7598
www.aarp.org

AARP is a nonprofit organization that advocates for older Americans' health, rights, and life choices. Local chapters provide information and services on crime prevention, consumer protection, and income tax preparation. Members can join group health, auto, life, and home insurance programs, investment plans, or a discount mail-order pharmacy service. Publications are available on housing, health, exercise, retirement planning, money management, leisure, and travel.

Health and Retirement Study
University of Michigan
Survey Research Center
PO Box 1248
Ann Arbor MI 48106-1248
(800) 759-7947
Spanish: (800) 643-7605
www.hrsparticipants.isr.umich.edu

The ongoing Health and Retirement Study provides researchers and policymakers unique long-term information about the lives and needs of people over 50 in the United States. They have more than ten years of data covering a multitude of subjects such as economic status, health insurance coverage, health status, work history, retirement plans, and family support.

National Council on Aging
300 D Street SW
Washington DC 20024
(202) 479-1200
TTY: (202) 479-6674
info@ncoa.org
www.ncoa.org

Founded in 1950, the National Council on Aging is an advocate for the elderly. Its member organizations include adult day service centers, employment services, senior housing, health centers, and congregate meal sites. The organization operates a website called BenefitsCheckUp.com, which allows users to search federal, state, and private benefit and prescription savings programs. Other programs include matching older volunteers with at-risk children and families as well as providing training and employment opportunities for older people.

Education

AARP, The Magazine (formerly Modern Maturity)
601 E Street NW
Washington DC 20049
(888) 687-2277
www.aarp.org

Travel service, real estate, well being, financial planning, and more.

Generations: Journal of the American Society on Aging
833 Market Street, Suite 511
San Francisco CA 94103
info@asaging.org
www.asaging.org

Covers the myriad issues facing those who are aging.

Kiplinger's Retirement Report
Kiplinger Washington Editors
1729 H Street NW
Washington DC 20006
(800) 544-0155
www.kiplinger.com

This report will provide you with authoritative help to plan and enjoy a worry-free retirement. It reveals the best strategies for retirement investing and estate planning, how to protect your nest egg and get the best health care, best ways to locate top retirement locations, secure the best housing, and more.

Mars Hill Audio
PO Box 7826
Charlottesville VA 22906-7826
(800) 331-6407
www.marshillaudio.org

Mars Hill audio tapes are a bimonthly audio magazine of contemporary culture and Christian conviction. Thinking people for thinking times. Outstanding interviews on significant issues in contemporary culture. (Highly recommended!)

Retirement Weekly
CBS MarketWatch
601 W 26th Street
New York NY 10001
(877) 870-0001
www.marketwatch.com/commerce/RetirementWeekly

As a subscriber, you'll receive actionable advice and guidance on
- techniques for saving for retirement without changing your lifestyle today
- how to build the best portfolio for long-term income

- how to make sure you don't outlive your income
- ways to get the most from tax laws
- Medicare
- vacation tips and other lifestyle features

The Teaching Company
4151 Lafayette Center Drive, Suite 100
Chantilly VA 20151-1232
www.teach12.com

Imagine if you could take only the courses that interest you most and have every course taught by one of America's greatest college lecturers from the country's premier universities—right in your own home or car! No homework, no exams. That is the breakthrough in lifelong learning that The Teaching Company has brought to thousands of knowledge-thirsty adult Americans since 1990. (Highly recommended!)

Third Age Universities
Find a local outlet by using your search engine to find "U3A." You will find many listings from around the world. (Information on Third Age Universities can be found in chapter 9 on page 200.)

Health-Related Issues

Alzheimer's Association
225 N Michigan Avenue, Suite 1700
Chicago IL 60601
(800) 272-3900
TTY: (312) 335-8882
www.alz.org

This nonprofit organization offers information and support services to people with Alzheimer's disease and their families. Contact the 24-hour, toll-free telephone line to link with local chapters and community resources. A free catalog of educational publications is available in English and Spanish.

American Association of Cardiovascular and Pulmonary Rehabilitation
401 North Michigan Avenue, Suite 2200
Chicago IL 60611
(312) 321-5145
www.aacvpr.org

AACPR is an organization of certified heart, lung, and blood specialists that provides information on diagnosis, treatment, and disease prevention. Information and publications are available on consumer guidelines for cardiac rehabilitation and purchasing fitness equipment. Visit the website for a free brochure.

American Foundation for Urologic Diseases
1000 Corporate Blvd, Suite 410
Linthicum MD 21090
(410) 689-3998
www.afud.org

This foundation works toward the prevention and cure of urologic disease in part by keeping patients, family members, and friends informed about these disorders, treatment options, and recent research findings. AFUD operates six national health education councils that distribute patient education materials on a variety of urologic topics. One of the links on their website leads to information on prostate health. Online publications are free; publications are available by mail for a fee.

Bariani Olive Oil
(415) 864-1917
Bariani@aol.com
www.barianioliveoil.com

(The only olive oil I will use. To me and my family, cold-pressed virgin olive oil is like medicine.)

Citizens for Health
5 Thomas Circle NW, Suite 500
Washington DC 20005
(202) 483-4344
info@citizens.org
www.citizens.org

A majority of Americans use natural and alternative health approaches. By acting together, we can become a powerful and permanent voice for our right to health choices, cost-effective solutions to the nation's health crisis, and safer approaches to food and water policies.

Dr. Anthony Mercola
1443 W. Shaumburg Road, Suite 250
Shaumburg IL 60194
www.mercola.com

Dr. Mercola offers a free, twice-weekly e-mail health newsletter.

National Cancer Institute
6116 Executive Boulevard, Room 3036A
Bethesda MD 20892-8322
(800) 422-6237
(TTY) (800) 332-8615
www.nci.nih.gov

NCI's website has extensive information on cancer prevention, treatment, statistics, research, clinical trials, and news. Contact them directly for answers to questions about cancer, help with quitting smoking, and other informational materials.

National Stroke Association
9707 East Easter Lane
Englewood CO 80112-3747
(800) 787-6537
www.stroke.org

This association provides information about stroke prevention, acute treatment, recovery, and rehabilitation to the public. NSA offers referrals to support groups, care centers, and local resources for stroke survivors, caregivers, and family members.

Parkinson's Support Groups of America
11376 Cherry Hill Road # 204
Beltsville MD 20705
(301) 937-1545
www.parkinsonsinfo.com

This group's website hosts Awakenings, an open forum for everyone involved with Parkinson's disease.

Rising Star LLC
(800) 690-9255
rays@risingstarlc.com
www.risingstarlc.com

A good source of unrefined virgin coconut oil or important probiotics.

Self-Help for Hard of Hearing People, Inc.
7910 Woodmont Avenue, Suite 1200
Bethesda MD 20814
(301) 657-2248
(TTY) (301) 657-2249

SHHH provides information and services for people who are hard of hearing, including assistance on education and legal issues. Local SHHH chapters can provide information on community references and referrals to specialists. A list of publications and materials is available.

Vita-Mix Total Nutrition Center

Vita-Mix Corporation
8615 Usher Road
Cleveland OH 44138
(800) 848-2649

(Take away my stove, take away my dishwasher, but I'd be lost without my Vita-Mix!)

Sports, Pastimes

American Contract Bridge League

2990 Airways Blvd
Memphis TN 38116-3847
(901) 332-5586
(800) 467-1623
www.acbl.org

Have fun playing the world's greatest card game. Put your skills into play for social pleasure or serious competition.

National Audubon Society

700 Broadway
New York NY 10003
(212) 979-3000
www.audubon.org

Audubon's members are dedicated to protecting birds, wildlife, and the environment, and they work with policymakers in Washington DC, state legislatures, and local governments across the country.

The National Bowling Association

377 Park Avenue South, 7th Floor
New York NY 10016
(212) 689-8308
www.tnbainc.org

The NBA is one of the three major amateur bowling organizations in the USA. It was founded in 1939 by African Americans and is open to all.

National Scrabble Association
Williams and Co.
PO Box 700
Greenport NY 11944
(631) 477-0033
www.scrabble-assoc.com

The NSA organizes and promotes a number of high-profile Scrabble championships and provides many resources, including recent press releases, player biographical information, general information about the NSA, and a brief history of the game.

National Senior Games Association
PO Box 82059
Baton Rouge LA 70884-2059
(225) 766-6800
nsga@nsga.com
www.seniorolympics.net

The National Senior Games Association is the national organization that spearheads the senior games movement, sanctioning and coordinating the efforts of senior games organizations across the country. It is a nonprofit organization that is dedicated to promoting healthy lifestyles for active adults 50 and over through education, fitness, and sport. It strives to be the premier organization in the world supporting active adult athletes.

United States Chess Federation
3054 NYS, Route 9W
New Windsor NY 12553
(845) 562-8350
www.uschess.org

The U.S. Chess Federation is the official sanctioning body for over-the-board tournament play in the USA. With over 90,000 members, it offers something for every player, from beginner to Grandmaster. In addition to rating tournaments, the USCF supports and promotes chess activities throughout the USA.

Travel

Access-Able Travel

(A service of AAA—check your local listings for an AAA office near you.)
www.access-able.com

Access-Able Travel offers barrier-free travel guides for various locations. They also have information and resources you need to know about travel with a special need, disability magazines, access guides for cities, resorts, and attractions, wheelchair or scooter rentals, accessible transportation, and more.

Cross-Culture

12 White Pine Road
Amherst MA 01002-3469
(800) 491-1148
travel@crosscultureinc.com
www.crosscultureinc.com

Cross-Culture provides small-group, all-inclusive cultural tours, special-interest tours, hiking programs, and educational cruises. Past travelers have said that they are happily exhausted by their full itineraries. This organization does not sell free time!

Elderhostel

11 Avenue de Lafayette
Boston MA 02111-1746
(877) 426-8056
registration@elderhostel.org
www.elderhostel.org

(See the information in chapter 9 on pages 199-200.)

Elder Treks

597 Markham St.
Toronto ON M6G 2L7
Canada
(800) 741-7956
www.eldertreks.com

ElderTreks is the world's first adventure travel company designed exclusively for people 50 and over. With 15 years of experience, it offers active, off-the-beaten-path, small-group adventures in more than 50 countries. Its all-inclusive land journeys focus on adventure, culture, and nature.

Good Sam Club
PO Box 6888
Englewood CO 80155-6888
(800) 234-3450
www.goodsamclub.com

The Good Sam Club got its start many years ago when a handful of RV owners put Good Samaritan bumper stickers on their rigs so fellow members would know they could get help on the road. From this small club they grew. In the early days, Good Sam members spread the word at RV parks and other club events. Soon everyone wanted to know how to get a Good Sam "smiling face" decal. Their primary goal remains the same as from those days: to make RVing safer and more enjoyable, and to save members money through club-endorsed benefits and services. They take seriously their responsibilities to the environment, the highways, and the park system.

Interhostel
University of New Hampshire
6 Garrison Avenue
Durham NH 03824
(800) 733-9753
(603) 862-1147 (outside the USA)
Interhostel@unh.edu
www.learn.unh.edu/interhostel/contact.html

Life begins at 50 for those who love to travel and learn about the cultures of different countries. Interhostel offers lots of opportunities to expand your horizons, with learning vacations around the globe and in the USA.

Off the Beaten Path Guides to Unique Places
The Globe Pequot Press
PO Box 480
Guilford CT 06437
www.globepequot.com

Check with your local bookstore to find a guide that covers your state.

Over the Hill Gang International
1820 W Colorado Avenue
Colorado Springs CO 80904
(719) 389-0022
info@othgi.com
www.othgi.com

Over the Hill Gang International offers unsurpassed camaraderie, outstanding discounts, and great trips for people 50 and over. They are enthusiastic, fun-loving people who enjoy sharing the experience of skiing and other outdoor activities with other physically active seniors.

Trailer Life
PO Box 422
Mt. Morris IL 61054
(800) 825-6861
www.trailerlife.com

Articles and information about life on the road.

Washington Post's International Information Online
The Washington Post Company
www.washingtonpost.com/wp-srv/inatl/front/htm

Volunteerism

Experience Corps
2120 L Street NW, Suite 400
Washington DC 20037
info@experiencecorps.org
www.experiencecorps.org

Experience Corps offers new adventures in service for Americans over 55. Now in 12 cities, Experience Corps works to solve serious social problems, beginning with literacy. Today more than 1300 Corps members serve as tutors and mentors to children in urban public schools and after-school programs, where they help teach children to read and develop the confidence and skills to succeed in school and in life.

Global Volunteers
375 E Little Canada Road
St. Paul MN 35117
(800) 487-1074
www.globalvolunteers.org

Global Volunteers has mobilized more than 16,000 volunteers on community development projects for one, two, or three weeks worldwide since 1984.

Habitat for Humanity International
Partner Service Center
121 Habitat Street
Americus GA 31709-3498
(229) 924-6935
publicinfo@hfhi.org
www.habitat.org

Habitat for Humanity International is a nonprofit, ecumenical Christian housing ministry. HFHI seeks to eliminate poverty housing and homelessness from the world, and to make decent shelter a matter of conscience and action. Habitat invites people of all backgrounds, races, and religions to build houses together in partnership with families in need.

Lion's Club International
300 W 22nd Street
Oak Brook IL 60523-8842
(630) 571-5466
www.lionsclubs.org

Nearly 1.4 million Lions members in 193 countries and geographic areas answer the needs that challenge the communities of the world. Lions tackle tough problems like blindness, drug abuse prevention, and diabetes awareness. Lions members—men and women—provide immediate and sustained relief in time of disaster and offer long-term assistance to those in need. Lions collect and recycle eyeglasses for distribution in developing countries and treat millions of people to prevent river blindness.

Medical Ministry International
USA Office
PO Box 1339
Allen TX 75013
(972) 727-5864
mmitx@mmint.org

Medical Ministry Canada Inc.
15 John Street North, Suite 301
Hamilton ON L8R 1H1
Canada
(905) 524-3544
mmican@mmint.org
www.mmiusa.org

Medical Ministry International provides opportunities to serve Jesus Christ by offering spiritual and physical health care to people in need. Their vision is to care annually for 100 million of the world's needy by the year 2050. They are committed to meet the need for medical care among the world's poor with lasting solutions through excellence in medicine, patient care, and health education. They organize short-term medical missions and establish and equip permanent medical centers. MMI is an interdenominational medical mission.

Peace Corps
1111 20th Street NW
Washington DC 20526
(800) 424-8580
24-hour job line: (800) 818-9579
www.peacecorps.gov

The Peace Corps is one of the world's most successful and respected development organizations. Part of the Peace Corps' success is due to the dedicated people who work behind the scenes to support the agency and the thousands of volunteers serving overseas. This includes providing program and medical support, recruiting new Peace Corps volunteers, managing overseas offices, and providing important administrative services.

SCORE (Service Corps of Retired Executives)
409 Third Street NW
Washington DC 20416
(800) 636-0425
www.score.org

SCORE, a group of "counselors to America's small business," is a nonprofit association that provides entrepreneurs with free, confidential, face-to-face and e-mail business counseling. Counseling and workshops are offered at hundreds of chapter offices nationwide by volunteers who are experienced entrepreneurs or corporate managers or executives.

Senior Corps
Retired & Senior Volunteer Program (RSVP)
Corporation for National and Community Service
1201 New York Avenue NW
Washington DC 20525
TTY: (202) 565-2799
www.webmaster@cns.gov

Through Senior Corps, nearly half a million Americans age 55 and older share their time and talents to help solve local problems. Among other ventures are grandparent and senior companion programs.

RSVP is part of Senior Corps, a network of national service programs that provides older Americans the opportunity to apply their life experience to meeting community needs. RSVP volunteers serve in a diverse range of non-profit organizations, public agencies, and faith-based groups. Among other activities, they mentor at-risk youth, organize neighborhood watch programs, test drinking water for contaminants, teach English to immigrants, and lend their business skills to community groups that provide critical social services.

Workamper News
709 West Searcy Street
Heber Springs AR 72543-3761
(501) 362-2637
info@workamper.com
www.workamper.com

Across America, from Maine to California, people are living and working at resorts and other desirable places, traveling in their recreational vehicles, and making money in the process. Many find their jobs with the aid of Workamper News, a bimonthly magazine that advertises part-time and full-time job openings in recreation, travel, and tourism.

Notes

Chapter 1—A Wake-Up Call

1. CBS MarketWatch, Inc. ran an ad for its *Retirement Weekly* magazine by stating, "Fact: 75% of baby boomers are not adequately preparing for retirement" (*USA Today*, July 23, 2004). On its website, *Retirement Weekly* states that only 20 percent of the baby boom generation has a company retirement plan, and even fewer are taking advantage of one. The other 80 percent are completely on their own. *US News and World Report* dedicated its June 14, 2004 issue to retirement. One feature writer indicated that "Americans are hardly saving anything; as many as 25 million boomers, or nearly one third, have virtually nothing saved for retirement; very few people can afford to live well on a fixed income for 15 or 20 years (Betsy Hammond, "Today's Retirement Journey"). In Kiplinger's *Retirement Planning: Your Guide to Securing Your Dreams*, Mary Beth Franklin states that only 42 percent of all workers have ever even tried to calculate how much money they need to set aside, and of those, more than 40 percent were shocked into increasing their savings. Four in ten workers are doing *nothing*, and many of the ones who are saving aren't saving enough.

2. "Linda Miller, Chicago, Illinois: Laid Off, Uninsured, Sick" *Parade* (August 15, 2004).

Chapter 2—What's It All About, Alfie?

1. Christine A. Price, "Facts About Retirement" (The Ohio State University Extension Senior Services). Dr. Price goes on to say, "With the creation of Social Security, a financial incentive or pension was made available to older workers to encourage them to retire from the workforce and to enable younger workers to take their place; thus stimulating economic growth and progress. This opportunity to 'retire' from paid employment provided older adults with a new lifestyle of a 'retiree.'"

Chapter 4—Financing Retirement or Retiring Finances?

1. Mary Beth Franklin, "A Moving Retirement," *Kiplinger's Retirement Planning,* Fall 2004, p. 115.

Chapter 7—What's a Body to Do?

1. "A Profile of Older Americans: 2002," Administration on Aging, U.S. Dept of Health and Human Services, p. 12.

Bibliography

Administration on Aging, US Department of Health and Human Services. "A Profile of Older Americans: 2002." www.aoa.gov/prof/Statistics/profile/1.asp.

Baker, Sidney MacDonald. *Detoxification & Healing: The Key to Optimal Health.* Columbus, OH: McGraw-Hill, 2003.

Beal, Flint, et al., eds. *The DANA Guide to Brain Health.* New York: Free Press, 2003.

Berry, Wendell. *The Art of the Commonplace.* Washington, DC: Shoemaker & Hoard, 2003.

————. *Sex, Freedom, and Community.* New York: Pantheon Books, 1993.

Brand-Miller, Jennie, et al. *The Glucose Revolution.* New York: Marlowe & Company, 1999.

Brodie, James Michael. "Impotence: Taking on the Old Taboo." *2004 Family Doctor.* American Academy of Family Physicians. Bastor Hannah International.

Carper, Jean. *Food: Your Miracle Medicine.* New York: HarperTorch, 1998.

Elwell, Walter A., ed. *The Evangelical Dictionary of Theology.* Grand Rapids: Baker Academic, 2001.

Franklin, Mary Beth. "A Moving Retirement." *Kiplinger Retirement Planning* (Fall, 2004).

Habermas, Gary R., and Moreland, J.P. *Immortality: The Other Side of Death.* Nashville: Thomas Nelson Inc., 1992.

Hales, Dianne, and Robert E. Hales. "Too Tough to Seek Help?" *Parade* (November 20, 2004).

Harrison, R.K., ed. *Encyclopedia of Biblical Ethics.* Rev ed. New York: Testament, 2003.

Howells, John. *Retirement on a Shoestring.* Guilford, CN: Globe Pequot, 2004.

Kanner, Bernice. *Are You Normal About Money?* New York: Bloomberg Press, 2001.

Karpel, Craig S. *The Retirement Myth.* New York: HarperCollins, 1995.

Kinkead, Gwen. "You Call This Retirement?" *US News and World Report* (June 14, 2004).

Nouwen, Henri J.M. *Here and Now: Living in the Spirit.* New York: Crossroad General Interest, 2002.

Sande, Ken. *The Peacemaker: A Biblical Guide to Resolving Personal Conflict.* Grand Rapids: Baker Books, 2004.

Schlossberg, Nancy K. *Retire Smart, Retire Happy.* Washington, DC: American Psychological Association, 2003.

Streisand, Betsey. "Today's Retirement Journey." *US News and World Report* (June 14, 2004).

Willis, Robert J. *Health and Retirement Study.* Ann Arbor, MI: University of Michigan Survey Research Center.

Yates, Cynthia. *Money and Me: A Woman's Guide to Financial Confidence.* Ann Arbor, MI: Servant Publications, 1999.

Other Good ——— Harvest House Reading

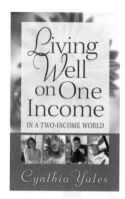

LIVING WELL ON ONE INCOME
Cynthia Yates

Cynthia Yates shows readers how to enjoy life more but spend less—on one income. Abundant personal stories, amusing anecdotes, and practical ideas invite you to a life of "one-income living with flair."

DITCH THE DIET AND THE BUDGET... AND FIND A BETTER WAY TO LIVE
Cynthia Yates

Who wouldn't like a little more money and a little less weight? With her trademark warmth, humor, and common sense, award-winning humor columnist Cynthia Yates points you to a better way to live.

MONEY MANAGEMENT FOR THOSE WHO DON'T HAVE ANY
Jim Paris

Financial counselor Jim Paris shares how readers can handle their money in a God-honoring way and enjoy the benefits of sound financial planning. This book contains more than 200 practical strategies to achieve financial success.

HARVEST HOUSE
PUBLISHERS